Keep Your Eye

on the

Prize!

A Young Person's Guidebook to Adulthood

Barbara Long, M.D., Ph.D.

Keep Your Eye

on the

Prize!

A Young Person's Guidebook to Adulthood

Barbara Long, M.D., Ph.D.

Copyright © 2011
All Rights Reserved

ISBN: 13-Digit: 978-1-59581-633-7
10-Digit: 1-59581-633-X

For additional copies, email Dr. Long at
barbaralongmdphd@gmail.com

PUBLISHED BY:
BRENTWOOD PUBLISHERS GROUP
4000 BEALLWOOD AVENUE
COLUMBUS, GEORGIA 31904

What they're saying about
Keep Your Eye on the Prize!

"Absolutely essential for anyone leaving home for the first time. Avoid this book at your peril. Read it, absorb it — and you'll never be stupid again!"

WINSTON GROOM, author of *Forrest Gump*

"This is an outstanding book for students entering college. It spells out typical psychological and social problems, guides the reader to understand underlying causes and mental mechanisms and gives superb direction in dealing with these problems. It is must reading for students and their counselors."

STEPHEN SCHEIBER, M.D.
Past Executive Vice-President, American Board of Psychiatry and Neurology
Past President, Group for the Advancement of Psychiatry, the profession's oldest "think tank"

"Dr. Barbara Long's book, *Keep Your Eye on the Prize!,* is a powerful addition to the literature. It provides a wealth of information for young people and those who counsel and interact with them. The book includes, as well as many other sections, a very understandable integration of psychodynamic concepts and real life experiences. Also a section on social networking and the Internet in today's world is very important with an understanding of feelings and behavior as they relate to this area and the important need for boundaries. The book has uplifting and valid information for all. I strongly endorse it."

MARCIA KRAFT GOIN, M.D., PH.D.
Past President, American Psychiatric Association
Professor of Clinical Psychiatry
Keck School of Medicine, University of Southern California

"Barbara Long's insightful book breaks new ground by examining the later years of adolescence and of early adulthood, rarely considered together. In today's world, that passage is ever more complex, and this work provides valuable insights, helpful reference materials, and compelling illustrations of the journey. Whether you are an adolescent, young adult, parent, educator, counselor, or clinician, you will be better informed, indeed strengthened, by this book."

LANCE ODDEN,
Headmaster Emeritus, The Taft School

"This good book written by Dr. Barbara Long is, in my opinion, a most useful and practical guide for young people. It is hard to be a young person these days, so to have wise and caring words of problem solving advice available in a pocket guide is wonderful. I wholeheartedly endorse this inspirational work which I believe will serve young people and their parents quite well."

FRANK D. MILLET
Director of Admission Emeritus, Milton Academy

"Keep Your Eye on the Prize! is an excellent guide for college-bound high school youth and their parents, but it also would be a valuable resource for educators and counselors. It explains the psychological constructs associated with the transition from adolescence to young adulthood in a refreshing literary style that uses case vignettes and information tools accompanying each chapter. I plan to add this "prize" to my library and anticipate I will be referring to it regularly."

BETH ANN BROOKS, M.D., M.S.A.
Professor and Associate Chair for Education
Wayne State University Department of Psychiatry
and Behavioral Neurosciences
Program Director, Psychiatry and
Child/Adolescent Psychiatry Residency Programs,
Detroit Medical Center/Wayne State University,
Director, American Board of Psychiatry and Neurology

"Going off to college is an exciting, challenging and at times stressful life-changing event. It is a transition that requires learning new psychological and interpersonal tools. Barbara Long's *Keep Your Eye on the Prize* is a clear and well-written "toolbox" that parents will want in their childrens' backpacks or e-book reader and that educators should share with their students."

JACK DRESCHER, MD
Clinical Associate Professor, New York Medical College
President-Elect, Group for the Advancement of Psychiatry
Emeritus Editor, Journal of Gay and Lesbian Mental Health

To R.W. L., who would have been tickled pink

ACKNOWLEDGEMENTS

The author gratefully acknowledges the following people, who offered invaluable input:

William Fitzsimmons, Dean of Undergraduate Admissions, Harvard College
Thomas Dingman, Freshmen Dean, Harvard College
Stephen Parker
Kathryn Long
Skip Issacs
Peter Reich, M.D.
Barrie Greiff, M.D.
David Adler, M.D.
Stewart Adelson, M.D.
Jack Drescher, M.D.
Marcia Goin, M.D.
Steve Scheiber, M.D.
Beth Ann Brooks, M.D.
Peter Zeman, M.D.
Carlene Elsner, M.D.
Winston Groom
Jeanne Phillips
John and Elizabeth Massey
John Patterson
Patty Burns
Jack Shaw

Bobby and Lynda Horton

Wade Boggs

Nancy Beane

Robert E. Lee IV

Frank Millet

Suzie Greenup

Lance Odden

Ashley Elsner

Heather Elsner

Elizabeth Coursen

Desmond Mitchell

JiHye Choi

Nicole Jameson

Charlita Lockett

Special thanks to Harrison Parker for the artwork and photography.

TABLE OF CONTENTS

Page

Foreword...*4*

Introduction..*7*

Chapter 1: The Transitional Years....................*9*
    Your Personal Prism *9*
    Style...*12*
    Identity...*15*
    Your Brain, You, and Your Parents *16*
    Sexuality and Sexual Orientation.............*21*

Chapter 2: Finding <u>Your</u> Pathway and Relating to Others.......*27*
    Going off of "Auto Pilot"...........................*27*
    Relating to Others—Growing from "I" to "We"...............*31*
        The Internet, Our Lives, and Relationships...............*34*
        Social Networking *41*

Chapter 3: Finding the Fit *54*

Chapter 4: The Big Picture *61*
    The 4 Compass Points of Life— Mental, Physical,
    Spiritual, Emotional *61*

Chapter 5: The Emotional Compass Point..................................71

   The Soul and the Emotions—Happiness and Pain............71

   Psychological Tasks of Life 72

   The Conscious and the Unconscious................................72

   The Role of the Defense Mechanisms................................81

   Encounter With the Shadow— Projecting the Negative 84

      A Word about the "Money Shadow" 89

   Falling in Love—Projecting the Ideal.............................92

   Reality Check—Difficult People and How They Act........99

      Acting Out..103

      Passive Aggressive Behavior.................................104

   Emotional Suffering 107

   Anxiety 107

   Shame and Humiliation 118

   Shame and the Issue of "Class" 125

   Jealousy and Envy—the Green-Eyed Monster................129

   Anger and Rage 135

   Loss...139

   Depression...142

      A Word about Suicide 145

Chapter 6: Super Strategies for Stormy Times 147

   Helping Others..147

   Humor...149

   Forgiveness 152

   "On One Hand"—Thanking Those Who Have Helped....156

Chapter 7: Sisyphus and the Problem of "Rowing Upstream" *160*

Chapter 8: The Miracle of Healing *165*

Chapter 9: Synchronicity *174*

Chapter 10: The Stumbles of Life *179*
   Independence and "Culture Shock" *179*
   Harming Others—Bullying and Hazing *184*
   Harming Yourself *188*
     Alcohol *188*
     Weight and Eating Disorders *193*
     Sexuality *198*
     Drugs *202*
     Self-Injury *204*

Chapter 11: Keep Your Eye on the Prize!
   Aim High, Play Fair, and Smell the Roses Along the Way....*206*

Appendix: Resources *217*

FOREWORD

My late father grew up in the country in "L.A.," "Lower Alabama." A powerful man from a colorful family, he was full of wisdom, but his favorite saying when I was growing up was "Keep Your Eye On the Prize!" Throughout life, I have kept his counsel in mind, focusing on the "big picture" and trying not to get side-tracked or derailed by the "little things," destructive relationships, or situations that I could not control or change. In addition to applying this motto to my personal life, I have shared it with students, patients, friends, family, and other people of all ages and walks of life.

I have always worked with young people in my clinical practice, but more than 30 years ago, I also began to interview students applying for undergraduate admission to a New England college. I have been privileged to keep up with many of these students. Most have done extraordinarily well in their adjustment to college. A few, however, have had difficulties, even suffering so much culture shock that they left the college or transferred to a school closer to home. Youth who chose to enter the world of work instead of college experienced the same adjustment issues as their peers who went to college.

As I watched these young people meet the challenges of their 20s, I wondered if my profession might have offered something to ease their transition. Were there any psychological tools that could have helped them to adjust to college and career—tools, in fact, that could apply, to all young people adjusting to adult life?

This book attempts to fill this need. It introduces some basic concepts about the psychological transformation that young people will experience over their late teenage years into their 20s and beyond. Packed with true stories (with identities disguised) and practical "tools" for handling problems, the book teaches some of the fundamentals of a good life and strategies for managing the emotions that accompany this growth process. Where appropriate, additional resources, such as websites, groups, and books are mentioned, although these references do not constitute an official "recommendation" or any guarantee that they will be useful in any individual situation. When in doubt, consult a parent, doctor, mental health counselor, or other trusted adult.

The book is a series of conversations that address core issues—conversations that a young person can have with himself or herself, or talks that he or she might have with a parent, older friend, teacher, mentor, doctor, aunt or uncle, clerical leader, school counselor, mental health counselor, or even grandparent. In fact, this book is an essential read for anyone who wants to reinforce those universal and never-changing core values that will help youth become happy, well-adjusted, and responsible adults in this complex and ever-changing world.

To all the young people who will read this book, I say, "Work hard, play fair, and take the high road in life!" To this my father would add, "Keep your roots but spread your wings, and always Keep Your Eye on the Prize!!"

INTRODUCTION

The mid-teens through the 20s are unlike any time before or after, a period of time from which you will emerge a different person —physically, intellectually, emotionally, and spiritually. How this change occurs is a mystery, but it does. Do you remember learning about chemistry? The processes that involved mixing substance A with substance B and getting substance C that was different from either A or B? Somehow the molecules of A and B rearranged themselves and became something totally different. This time period creates the same kind of transformational process, mixing you (substance A) with the college or work environment (substance B) and producing C, a new person that has been "rearranged" to be an adult. Not unlike what happened in the chemistry lab, some of the change occurs abruptly, while most of it occurs more gradually. All of it involves a tremendous amount of learning—not only the book type of learning, but also the psychological and emotional kind.

Most people go through this experience without thinking much about what is happening. They bring with them whatever psychological and coping strategies they developed in childhood and high school. When problems arise, the tools acquired from the past may not be very helpful. Coping could be much easier if there were some new tools, more suited to this new chapter of life. This pocket guide will give you new ones that you can add to your toolkit of life, drawing from stories, suggestions, and new ways of thinking and solving problems. Keep these tools in the back pocket of your mind as you embark on your journey!

There are four main phases in this time of life:

1. *Transition from High School*
2. *Adjustment*
3. *Transformation*
4. *Resolution and Maturity as an Adult*

To get from Phase 1 to Phase 4 does not happen overnight or even in a year. Like a house is built one brick at a time, a life is built one day at a time. This book will help you enter the Transition, learn about the Adjustment, and maximize the positive changes of the Transformational phase. With these tools, you will become the mature, unique, and happy adult you are meant to be. You will know you have gotten to the final chapter, Resolution, when you take stock of your life and find you have meaningful work, reliable friends (and, if you want it, a family), and a life purpose that benefits others. When you read this book, some chapters may immediately resonate with you, while others will not. That's okay. Read them over lightly for now but keep them in your back pocket. Later, they may "hit home" with what is going on in your life, and you can take another look. Building a life is like building a house. The more tools you have available to use, the stronger your house will be, so let's get going with your life!

- *Chapter One* -

The TRANSITIONAL YEARS

You are finishing or have already finished high school and are ready for the next chapter of your life. Over the next few years, you will grow and change a lot, make relationships, and get going on a career. Welcome to the *Transitional* years! Most people find this to be a *great*, even *magical*, time of life —full of growth, exploration, joy, and just plain fun. Enjoy these years and learn all you can about yourself, and you will gain the skills and confidence to lead a successful and happy life. This chapter will talk about five fundamental ideas—your *Prism, Style, Identity, Brain,* and *Sexuality and Sexual Orientation.*

YOUR PERSONAL PRISM

You look at the world and everything around you through your own *prism*—your unique perspective that comes partly from your genes and partly from past experiences and relationships with others. The more you understand about your prism, the more you can build the confidence you will need to manage relationships and solve problems. Let's look at how you can examine the *prism*.

Think about how your life experiences have determined who you are and how you see the world. Those experiences include messages you received from others—family, friends, school, community, and strangers. You absorbed these experiences and messages into your emotional makeup, often without question. Some messages may have been positive and boosted your self-esteem: "You are brilliant" (or talented). Others may have been not so flattering: "You are "stupid" (or lazy or selfish). What messages about yourself did you accept from others?

There were also ideas you developed about yourself—what kind of person you are and what expectations you have about yourself and the world. These, too, can be positive or negative, realistic or unrealistic, giving a light or dark cast to the prism. "I am the best" (or the worst). "I have to be perfect" (or "make A's, be cool, be thin, please my parents, get into college, get a relationship.") What ideas about yourself did you develop?

Genetics, past experiences, and our own ideas about ourselves blend together to make us optimistic or pessimistic when problems arise. If you are an optimist, you will think, "I won't let this

10

get me down — everything will turn out okay." If you are more of a pessimist, you will be more uncertain: "If I fail, I am worthless." "Nothing ever seems to turn out right for me." Which are you?

As you go along, get to know your *prism*. Examine your assumptions about the world and yourself, as these will color everything you do. Are your expectations of yourself and the world overly negative or positive? An overly negative view can defeat you and add more difficulty to a situation than it deserves! An overly positive view can lead to disappointments again and again. This is the time of life when you can "rebalance" your expectations of yourself and the world and reconstitute that *prism*!

⚒ Tools:

1. Make a list of terms that best describe first, how you feel about yourself, and second, how you feel about trying out new situations.

2. Now, try these experiments:

   A. You are preparing something for school or work. As you do this, tell yourself that you will do the best you can, and no matter what the outcome, you will learn something useful. And guess what? Maybe your best is pretty darn good. A wise doctor realized as a young man: "I'm just as good as the next guy, and in some areas, maybe a little bit better!"

B. As you enter a new situation or meet new people, don't automatically assume the best or the worst about them. Try for a "neutral" stance and tell yourself you will make a judgment about it later. Then take some time to evaluate it, and don't make a snap decision.

STYLE

Just as the *prism* colors our attitude toward ourselves and the world, there is another factor that also determines how we interact with others. This is your *personality style*, and it is important to learn as much as you can about it. For example, if your style is "extroverted," you will enthusiastically enter new social situations, but if it is "introverted," you will tend to shy away from them. For example, you're invited to a party. The *extrovert* says, "I love going to parties and meeting new people!" Or you're about to meet your new roommates. The extrovert will say, "I can't wait to move into my new room and meet them!" The *intro-*

vert says, ""I don't care for parties; I hate having to make superficial conversation!" Introverts may prefer single rooms, but if they are going to have roommates, they are likely to say, "I hope they work out okay."

Although America tends toward extroversion, neither style is "better" than the other; they just are what they are. Both styles have strengths and weaknesses and create different expectations. Extroverts tend to get into lots of situations, some good and others not so good, so they need to develop a bit of caution to avoid danger. The introvert, who is more reserved, reluctant, or apprehensive, needs to step out and take a few chances! And guess what? You never know what will happen. The extrovert may not enjoy the new experience at all, while the introvert may be surprised and delighted by the experience and may meet the love of his or her life, or, if not a lifelong love, someone who can give friendship or companionship or open doors to new activities or ideas.

✷ *Tools:*

1. To all you extroverts and introverts: Situations and people will rarely turn out to be as *good* or as *bad* as you think, so, as with the prism, try for a "neutral" stance and be open to being surprised. To you introverts: Believe it or not, the more you do, the more fun you have, so take a chance and step out!

13

2. Not sure about your style? There is a psychological instrument that can tell you about it. It is called the Myers-Briggs Type Indicator® (MBTI®), and it was developed by Isabel Briggs Myers based on the work of the Swiss psychologist, Carl Jung. The MBTI® describes four axes, or pairs of contrasting personality characteristics, of which extroverted/ introverted is just one. If you search "Myers-Briggs" on the Internet, you can learn more about this instrument. Here are the Four Axes:

Extroverted .... Introverted
Sensing.. Intuitive
Thinking ....Feeling
Judging..Perceptive

3. Remember that everyone has some of each characteristic. No one is a "pure" example of any of these traits, but most people have preferences on each axis. Consider taking the MBTI® to learn more about your style. This will help you relate better to others by understanding yourself and them better. It can also help you to think about a career that is a good fit for your "type."

IDENTITY

It may not be easy to imagine now, but you will look back at these years as the time when you forged the major pieces of your *identity*—that core of your being that defines who you are. Some of these pieces include sexual role as male or female, sexual orientation, career path, ethics and values, and artistic, political, community, and social interests, to name a few. You already have some pieces in place from the past. Keep what is good and build on that foundation, but as you explore different aspects of life, things may shift as you enlarge your perspective. You will confront a host of choices and make decisions about how you define yourself and conduct your life. Some of these will be easy, while others may be more challenging.

As you go along, you will also probably shed some misconceptions about yourself—ideas that needed updating, something like a software "upgrade." Other people can teach us a lot about ourselves, helping smooth our rough edges and pushing us to change. These are adjustments we need to make in order to learn how to behave in a way that is assertive without being demanding, honest without being injurious, helpful without losing our own boundaries, inquisitive without being invasive, and cooperative without allowing ourselves to be exploited.

YOUR BRAIN, YOU, and YOUR PARENTS

Establishing your *identity* and *independence* can make these years an *emotional roller coaster*, for you, your parents, peers, teachers, and the other adults in your life. In the past, we thought that all the problems between teens and adults (especially their parents) had to do with teens being obnoxious and defiant on purpose. Now we are learning from the ever-evolving field of *neuroscience* that part of what makes this a challenging time has to do with normal growth and development taking place in your brain—development that will continue until well into your 20s, at least. These changes are both chemical and structural, making your brain like a house that is constantly "under construction." We'll talk about three key changes, but check out this program, "Inside the Teenage Brain," which will tell you more:

http://www.pbs.org/wgbh/pages/frontline/shows/teenbrain/view/#rest

The **first** change involves your sleep cycle, which, in contrast to an adult's, is "phase-shifted," meaning that you will naturally prefer to stay up late and sleep in. The hormone, melatonin, which makes us naturally sleepy, is involved in this shift, not establishing an adult pattern until later. Because of this phase shift, you probably find it hard to get up in the morning, get yourself together, and make it to school on time, much less stay awake during those early morning classes! However, late at night, when your parents and teachers are asleep, you are wide awake and at your best. This makes for a hard week, in which you become increasingly

16

sleep-deprived, and by the weekend, you are really exhausted and just want to catch up on your sleep. Why does this matter?

Research has found that sleep is involved in learning, organizing, and retaining new information. In a survey of 3000 high-school students, researchers Amy R. Wolfson, Ph.D. and Mary A. Carskadon, Ph.D.[1] found that students who reported getting C's, D's and F's got about 25 minutes less sleep and went to bed about 40 minutes later than students who reported getting A's and B's, so sleep deprivation seems to go along with poorer grades. Concentration, learning, memory, and mood are all affected by sleep, and students who are sleep-deprived are also at risk for auto accidents. How much sleep do you need? Studies show that teens need at least *9* hours of sleep a night. *"Are you kidding?!"* I can hear you say. So the problem goes on: you need the sleep to function, but your body is out of sync with the schedule society has established for you. Is there anything you can do about this? See *Tool #1* below.

A **second** change involves growth of the part of the brain that helps us control our emotions, delay before acting, understand the possible effects of what we say and do, strategize, and handle the complexities of information we have to deal with in order to make good decisions and take appropriate action.

---

[1] Cited in article, "Sleep deprivation may be undermining teen health," by Siri Carpenter (staff member), in American Psychological Association Monitor, October 2001, Vol. 32, No. 9, p. 42. See http://www.apa.org/monitor/oct01/sleepteen.aspx

These are the "executive functions" that will help us organize our lives and reach our full potential as adults. While this part of the brain is growing, it is also mostly "off line" to help us think and plan before we act, while the brain's instinctive, gut-level emotional centers tend to be in charge. Because of this, you may find that you feel keyed up emotionally a lot of the time—angry and/or sexually aroused, on top of the world, or in the pits—and you may act on your feelings impulsively, rather than delay and think about the possible consequences, only to feel regretful later. The good news is that over time, as the executive centers of the brain mature, it will get easier to handle emotions, but here's a cautionary note: these crucial functions can be permanently damaged by drugs, alcohol, and accidents (See Chapter 10).

A **third** finding is that during these years, the brain adds a lot of new cells while discarding past brain-encoded experiences no longer used. New pathways are constructed based on your genes and the experiences you have at this time. The good news is that if you "messed up" in the past, you can turn over a new leaf and get on the right track, but here's a cautionary note: according to brain research, whatever you do with your time **now** can have *permanent* effects on your brain, because these experiences become new pathways that you will use for the rest of your life. Do you text or Facebook non-stop? If so, your social skills are apt to be whittled away, while your brain (and your life) becomes ever more self-absorbed. Are you spending time learning a sport, acting in plays, interacting with your peers, or tutoring other kids?

Don't minimize these socially interactive pursuits, because you will use and enjoy these skills and interests throughout life!

⚒ Tools:

1. Can you adjust your sleep cycle, so that you are not exhausted all the time? Here's a tip from people who have to fly across time zones. They accommodate to the time changes by resetting their biological clocks in advance. Because your body gets used to your sleep pattern of going to sleep and waking up at certain times, you can "train" it to go to sleep a little earlier so you don't get so tired during the week. But the bad news is that in order for this to work, you have to be rigid in this training process (including weekends) if you want your brain to accept a schedule it does not naturally want! Try going to bed 15 minutes earlier every few days while you get up at the same time. This may make it a little easier to get up during the week. Also see the discussion about l-tryptophan and serotonin, natural substances that help sleep and relaxation (Chapter 5, *Tool #1* under the "Anxiety" section, page 113).

2. Since you are "constructing" the brain you will have for life, go for all of the positive constructive experiences you can have! Take advantage of all the great activities that your school and community offer—classes, sports, art, music, drama, volunteer opportunities, and school and community clubs and groups. Through these activities, you will develop life-long interests, friends, and skills.

3. Although you are establishing your own identity, stay in communication with your parents, as this is a relationship for the long haul. You can't trade them in for a different model, and in life, you will need all the support you can get.

4. Monitor your emotions and work on modulating them while your brain is strengthening the areas that will help you to do this. (See the "Emotions Scale," p. 88; also section on "Anger and Rage" and its Tools.) This is the time to learn how to think before you speak and act. If you find yourself out of control— yelling at your parent, talking back to a teacher, or even getting into physical fights,

swing into *damage control* by first taking a break. After you cool off, talk about your feelings with your parents or another adult friend. Learn how to apologize (this is the damage control) and work on controlling your behavior. **Words matter and can hurt.** Your parents love you and want to help and support, so give them a chance rather than push them away.

5. Parents— work on those buttons your teen is pushing and avoid retaliation when you are angry. Your teen is learning self-control. Show them how to communicate anger appropriately and avoid damaging the relationship yourself! Most of all, make time to listen, and be there when your teen wants to talk. Don't let these moments of connection pass—they will never come again.

SEXUALITY and SEXUAL ORIENTATION

Our sexuality and sexual orientation, important pieces of who we are, mature and develop during the Transition years. Although growing into sexual maturity will be stormy for nearly everyone at times, most young people adjust well, integrating sexuality and sexual orientation into the larger fabric of their lives. Whether their sexual feelings are intense or subdued, they learn to manage them appropriately. Since a large majority of humans are heterosexual, most young people will assume gender roles without having to think a great deal about it. For others in the minority, however, including youth who are unsure about their sexual orientation, or who struggle with patterns of sexual arousal and sexual fantasies pointing to a possible gay, lesbian, or bisexual (GLB) sexual orientation, the Transition years may be confusing or filled with shame and guilt about not fitting into the usual sexual orientation role. Emotions can run high, leading some of these youth to be at risk, especially those who may have a same-sex experience before he or she has inwardly accepted a gay identity.

There is another group, who may feel as though they are trapped in the body of the wrong sex. These "transgender" (T) youth have an intense desire to be the opposite sex. For them, this can also be a time of questions and distress as they struggle with the idea of "gender non-conformity."

Some questioning youth (Q) in the Transition period will continue to question for a number of years, never really being able to sort out if they are straight or gay. Some who question may turn out to be straight, while others will accept a gay identity. Whether they are QGLB or gender non-conforming, these young people may feel isolated and lonely and have difficulty visualizing anything but continuing pain in adult life. Research has shown that QGLB and gender non-conforming youth are more likely than their heterosexual counterparts to be disparaged, harassed, or even punished by peers. If you come from more limited means or are of certain ethnic, cultural, and religious backgrounds, the potential for harassment based on sexual orientation can be worse. It is unclear how much discrimination happens because those with gender variance present themselves in a way that is "different" than the majority, and how much relates to their sexual orientation. But what is clear is that QGLB or gender non-conforming youth can be at risk for drug abuse, self-destructive behaviors such as burning or cutting, promiscuity, depression, anxiety disorders, and suicide. If you are struggling with sexuality and gender variance issues, here are some tools.

✗ Tools:

1. You are not alone. There are many supportive, successful, and well-adjusted GLBT adults who can help you through this time. They will tell you that if you can get through these years, life will improve. In fact, there is an excellent film that you should see. Go to **www.thetrevorproject.org** and look at the YouTube entitled, "It Gets Better." While you are on their website, check out the Trevor Project's resources to connect to supportive GLBT adults who can pro-

vide emotional support, advice, and a nurturing context for growing a healthy sexual identity.

2. <u>Being GLBQ or gender-non-conforming does not mean you are mentally ill, have poor judgment, or are destined to have problems in life!</u> Today, more than ever before, you have the prospect of living a fulfilled, happy, and well-balanced life.

3. Do not assume that because of your sexual orientation, everyone is against you. Many report that others had no problem accepting them. Get plugged into a supportive social group and enjoy being who you are!

4. While you find others who share your sexual orientation, find things you enjoy doing and develop friends who share your broader interests. Remember that sexuality is only one of a variety of factors that defines who you are.

5. Coming out can be a private, often difficult issue, and GLBTQ youth, like everybody else, want and need support from peers. Be cautious about

"coming out" online and revealing too much of yourself in social networking groups or blogs. Some youth assume that this is a safe, anonymous environment in which they will find support. Although many build bridges through online connections, for others, this has backfired, and they have suffered. The key is to connect to safe, healthy, and supportive online resources. One positive student group is the Gay Lesbian Straight Education Network (GLSEN). Their website is: **www.glsen.org.**

6. If you are unsure and/or struggling with your feelings in this area, consider counseling, which can help you deal with your feelings while you are sorting things out.

7. If you are getting into destructive activities like drugs, alcohol, burning, cutting, promiscuity, skipping school, or running away, or if you are feeling depressed, anxious, or even suicidal, see this as a call to action. Call the **Trevor Project Suicide Help Line at 866-488-7386.** They have a 24/7 crisis line designed to end suicide among GLBT youth. Reach out to GLSEN or

find a therapist through the gay and lesbian networks of the American Psychiatric Association (**www.psych.org**), American Psychological Association. (**www.apa.org**), or the Group For the Advancement of Psychiatry's LGBT Committee, which is a leader in this field (**www.ourgap.org** – click on the LGBT Committee link **www.aglp.org/gap**). They understand and are waiting to help you.

- *Chapter Two* -

FINDING <u>YOUR</u> PATHWAY
and
RELATING TO OTHERS

GOING OFF OF "AUTO PILOT"

Carl Jung observed that within all cultures, there is a kind of "herd mentality" or a "group-think" that people accept as the norm without question. People in this "collective unconscious" mindset are on "auto pilot" in life, flowing along and accepting without question the values and behavior dictated by the group. Do you remember this from school? Did you feel pressure to "go along" with the "cool crowd" in order to be accepted, even though this may not have been entirely comfortable? Did you feel that you were in a box that was not entirely of your own making? Well, now you have a choice.

Jung encouraged us to step out of this box into the world of possibilities and decide in a conscious way how we wish to live. According to Jung, the goal of life is *individuation*, a process that results in our becoming the unique person we truly are. M. Scott Peck, M.D. called this taking the *road less traveled*. See the Transition as your time to *individuate*—to find your own road that will take you down the life you are meant to enjoy!

But how do you get onto your *true pathway* rather than a *false* one? Finding your own path and not getting sidetracked onto someone else's can be tricky, as circumstances and important relationships can influence us to make choices we later reject. However, while this is a good time to "think out of the box," it does not make sense to dive into weird or destructive activities just for the sake of being different! Instead, just adopt a flexible mindset, recognizing that there are many useful and joyful ways to live life. You can accept some ideas and discard others that do not "fit." At the end of this trying out process, you may decide that you fit best with the collective culture and values around you, and that is fine too. The idea is to make this decision in a *conscious* way that will leave you feeling good about yourself and life!

Fundamental to this process are the *core values* that you will assemble. Test your beliefs in order to learn which ones to save and which to discard. Stick to them when you have to solve a problem in your life. At the same time, accept that others may believe differently. Don't let that make you fearful. Holding to our own principles when everyone around us disagrees can be hard on our self-esteem. Build a social support system of those who share your core beliefs, so that you do not feel alone.

Supportive friends can give us the courage to reflect on opposing arguments, while we make our own decisions, understanding that someone else's viewpoint may be *different*, but not necessarily *better* than ours. Although it can feel threatening to hear radically different views, they can also help us clarify our own beliefs. And remember, too, that freedom of conscience and expression are important American values, and tolerance and respect must go both ways. Just as you expect others to accept and respect your beliefs even if they don't share them, you should accept and respect theirs, and their right to express their ideas.

Work on accepting criticism, which can be instructive, if not so easy to take. Try to hear it without letting it diminish your self-esteem or make you feel personally attacked or somehow bad or inferior. The same is true of rejection. It hurts, but you have to keep it in perspective. After all, where is it written that everyone has to like us? Everybody has been rejected by someone. So try not to dwell on it or allow it to erode your self-esteem. Learn what you can from the experience and move on.

✗ Tools:

1. Dare to turn off the "auto Pilot" and step out of the collective unconscious. There are an infinite number of ways to live a great life. Find your own "true" pathway—individuate!

2. Here is a way to keep track of where you are going in your life. Make a list of things that you want to accomplish in one year and five years. When the year is up, revisit your list. See how many of the one-year aims you have accomplished and examine how you have progressed toward the longer-range goals. Then rethink your lists and your plans. Almost certainly, you will find that you have changed your mind about some goals and have others to add. And you should have new ideas about how to achieve the things that remain on your list. Adjust your goals and plans and set out again to achieve them.

3. Being true to yourself can sometimes leave you questioning what you are doing, especially if you

have moved away from the collective. Don't let these questions harm your self-esteem. Be tolerant of others, but stay on your pathway. Choose to be with people who enhance, rather than diminish, your sense of self.

4. Try this brief Self Esteem Assessment tool to see how you are doing in this area:

http://www.performancesolutions.nc.gov/ developmentInitiatives/CareerDevelopment/ Assessments/self-esteemassesment.aspx

5. A good self-esteem is based on values of responsibility and honor. Be a person others can count on to keep your promises. Once you lose your credibility with someone, it is next to impossible to get it back. If you have a duty to perform, go ahead and do it the best you can whether you want to or not.

RELATING TO OTHERS—Growing from "I" to "We"

The journey of life takes us through many phases. The teenage and young adult years involve rapid physical, intellectual, and psychological growth, as we shift from the physical, mental, and emotional makeup of a child to that of an adult. We discussed the changes in the brain in Chapter 1. Just as our bodies and brains grow, our perspective on life becomes more mature too, with a deeper grasp of the many complexities of human experience.

The perspective of an infant is unconscious and self-absorbed. It focuses on "I" with little awareness of others except its mother or another primary caretaker. As childhood progresses, we shift to a focus on "They," evaluating ourselves according to the standards of others. This is a linear, two-dimensional view that involves us and another person. We seek approval from our parents, teachers, coaches, or other adults and want them to approve of us and what we do. We work hard for good grades or an outstanding athletic or artistic performance. The grades and other rewards that we get boost our self-esteem, confidence, and motivation to continue our efforts.

The "They" perspective continues into adult life, as we seek to please partners, friends, and bosses. That is certainly appropriate and socially useful. But this perspective has its limitations. It has to be kept in proper proportion, or it can have a negative side. If we put too much importance on others' opinions, our self-esteem can suffer when they reject us or are critical of us or our actions. We can become so caught up in how others see us that we lose our internal sense of self—our values and sense of worthiness as a person. That can make us discouraged, depressed, and sometimes angry. Our anger may be directed at the other person who has found fault with us, or it may be directed at ourselves in self-critical regrets about our failures and shortcomings. To avoid getting stuck in this negative cycle, if something makes you feel criticized, unappreciated, or unvalued, work to understand what happened and try to use your disappointment constructively. Sooner or later everyone will come up against the limits of the "They" perspective. The task then is to grow beyond it—to the perspective of "We."

When we embrace the "We" point of view, we are able to evaluate our lives, actions, abilities, and limitations realistically according to the core values that we have developed and integrated into our lives. We take a multi-dimensional view of life. We measure our actions against our own internal standards while recognizing the views of others and accepting their criticisms. We are able to learn from differing perspectives without their diminishing our self-esteem or fostering feelings of failure or inferiority. We see ourselves as part of a complex web of relationships with others. If others reject us, we put this rejection into context, accepting that the other person sees things differently, but that his viewpoint is not necessarily more valid than ours.

The Internet, Our Lives and Relationships

The Internet has revolutionized the way we learn and relate to others. Never before has so much information been available so quickly— answering questions as quickly as we can enter them into a search engine. In the past, we could manage relatively simple combinations of tasks at the same time, such as listening to music while we worked out. Now we have become the ultimate multi-taskers, finding ourselves juggling many more tasks simultaneously, or at least *trying to*.

How the Internet is affecting our lives and our relationships remains controversial. As we access a universe of information, our brain activity increases as does our speed and skill in multi-tasking. For those in the arts, this has opened up exciting opportunities to create and innovate, while for others, computer simulations and games are a way to hone the physical and mental skills needed to operate complex machines, from airplanes to fighter drones used by the military.

But there are also potential risks, among them how to manage "information overload." While our brains try to accomplish one job, like homework, they are constantly being alerted to other activities, most of which are irrelevant, but often much more entertaining and emotionally satisfying than the task at hand! Who wouldn't rather see that fun YouTube or read an email from a long-lost friend than complete an assignment that feels boring? So many of us shuttle back and forth between the work we have to do and a multitude of distractions—tweets, instant messages, group chats, and email— and then find ourselves short on time and stressed out. All this multi-tasking can be difficult, as these two students discovered:

Subhash, a senior in high school, reported, "I tried to read the chapter of the book assigned for class while I checked my email, Facebook, and tweets. When a friend posted a YouTube clip, I clicked on it, because I knew it would be fun. And I found a program on computer animation and film-making, which, honestly, I would rather do than anything. I tried to do some of this while reading the book and chatting online with friends. But with all that switching back and forth, I found that when I returned to the book, I had lost my place and completely forgotten what I had read, so I had to start all over again. When my grades fell, I realized that I had dropped the ball. I was procrastinating and even forgetting to get schoolwork done, so I was doing it at the last minute before class and turning in sloppy shallow work that was full of errors. I was also tired all the time because I was on Facebook late at night talking with friends. Sometimes I had problems sleeping because my mind was so active or a message from a friend upset me a little. My parents were concerned about how much time I was spending online and asked me about it, but I was never honest with them. We had a long talk about my priorities. Finally, I had to force myself to look at reality. I wanted to do well in school, but there was not enough time for study and all the computer stuff. I made myself focus, first, on getting my work done. I set aside a specific time to catch up with friends but not late at night. It was really hard, as I felt like I was in withdrawal from a drug—missing out on what was going on with my friends and not doing as much animation as I wanted. But I wanted to do well in school, so I had to rethink my priorities and learn to manage time. The good news is my friends adjusted to my not being available all the time, I slept better, and my grades improved."

Mira, a community college student, found that she, too, was getting swept up in too much computer activity. "The computer was my great escape from reality, including my parents' divorce. It was easy, because there was a never-ending online drama going on with my friends. I couldn't tear myself away from it even for holidays or a vacation. If I could not check in with my friends online, I got anxious or down, and I even found that it was easier to be with them online than get together in real life. Plus, sitting at my computer all day, I had no time to work out and gained 20 pounds, just as if I was eating chocolate all the time. My friends complained that I never had time for them anymore, and when I did get together with them, I was snappy and hard to be around. One friend got really mad at me for texting while we were having lunch. She told me that I was as rude as those people that talk on the cell phone while on the cardio machines in the gym! That's when I told myself that things were *really* out of control, and only I could get my life back in order!"

Brain scientists are finding significant evidence that confirms what Subhash and Mira discovered. Because the Internet promotes and rewards this multi-tasking brain function, we may be "dumbing down" our brains, becoming too easily distracted, reducing our conversations to "tweets," and hampering our ability to focus, concentrate, reflect, retain information, grasp complicated ideas or factual knowledge, and analyze complex topics in depth. Procrastination, forgetfulness, impatience, and Internet-driven "attention deficit disorder" may be byproducts of uncontrolled Internet use, along with an unhealthy tendency to focus on ourselves, with minute to minute life updates that others really don't need to know and probably would rather not get! And along with difficulty in shutting down our brains for rest, these can lead to problems and stress in school, at work, or in personal relationships—problems that can be life-long, if these are the habits we form in our teens and 20s.

✷ Tools:

1. To find out if non-stop computer-generated activity is becoming an unhealthy stress in your life, you can answer some questions that are posed by New York Times health blogger, Tara Parker-Pope[1]

[1]See in
http://topics.nytimes.com/top/features/timestopics/series/your_brain_on_computers/index.html?scp=3&sq=Tara%20Parker%20Pope&st=cse, look under "Warning Signs of Tech Overload"

A. Do others complain about the amount of time you spend using technology?

B. Does going online lift you from depression or a nervous mood?

C. Do you choose to go online rather than go out with others?

D. Have you lied or tried to hide how long you've been online?

E. When you are online and someone needs you, do you say, "Just a few more minutes," before stopping?

F. Do you anticipate the next time you will be online?

G. Do you always check your email before doing other things?

2. If you said yes to any of these, it may be time to make some adjustments. This is simply common sense. If you overeat, you will get health problems. If you over-use technology, your physical and mental health may suffer along with your relationships.

3. In some ways, the Internet is no different than past technologies, like automobiles, telephones, and television, which can distract us and consume our time. Set priorities and focus on one task at a time. Don't allow yourself to procrastinate. Find a quiet place to study away from the computer or other distractions.

4. Set specific time limits on checking email, Facebook, and other sites. Try this: set aside 30 minutes only at certain times of the day, like morning, afternoon, and early evening, then re-orient your friends' expectations, letting them know you are otherwise "offline."

5. Remember in Chapter 1 when we talked about how your habits now become permanently grooved

into your brain? Go for fitness, emotionally, mentally, and physically. Turn off the computer, go outside, and make dates to get together with friends, and when you are with them, turn off your phone or Blackberry and give your attention to the people you are with.

6. While you are learning good life habits, get in your workout, run, tennis or basketball game, dance, do art, take a part in a play, volunteer, or go on a walk. Try a class in yoga, Tai Chi, or meditation to calm the mind.

7. At night your brain needs to gear down in order to sleep. Avoid engaging in online activities that can wait until the next day. Try reading a book — an activity that lets you sink in and lose yourself in a story or idea without being constantly pulled off into something else, so it is a good way to relax your mind and body. It is a great hobby and will help your attention span, concentration, and ability to follow and analyze ideas — skills you will need throughout life.

Social Networking

In addition to information, the Internet has also given us an electronic world of social connections through email and social networking websites. These resources can help us accumulate "social capital" by building bonds of emotional support and bridges of information exchange. This aspect of the Internet landscape is constantly changing, giving us new opportunities and challenges, so this section will only highlight some themes and give some general guidelines.

The potential good of cyber communication is huge. It can help us find old friends, maintain contacts and communication, find others with similar interests, work effectively with others on a common project, and discover new opportunities, such as jobs, membership organizations, or educational programs. Some people find that it enhances, rather than diminishes relationships.

But as with everything else in life, the positives are balanced with potential pitfalls in relying on the Internet as our major social outlet. As Subhash and Mira found, Internet socializing can consume large amounts of time, *feel* addictive (even if technically, it is not), and interfere with our relationships unless we set aside time for them. They learned that online relating robs us of face-to-face communication and body language—two essential ways that people communicate emotions, learn about others, and strengthen bonds. And as some young people have learned, social networking sites can make it easy for someone to dis-

seminate malicious or harmful content but hard to end relationships and forget about past mistakes.

Other effects may be more subtle. As one popular 20 year old
young woman observed, "Everyone is connected; everyone is
alone—the more connected, the lonelier." Some people come to
believe that they have thousands of other "friends," but these
may, in fact, be illusory. Even among young people who have
real, rather than just virtual, friends, socializing mostly through
the Internet may be changing the way we relate to others. One
change may involve our ability to tune in to or empathize with
others. For example, some users become excessively self-pre-
occupied, providing constant updates about their lives. They
perceive that others want to hear these minute-by-minute
accounts, even though they don't, but the updaters never get
this feed-back. Learning to balance *talking* about ourselves with
listening to others is a skill we acquire through many face-to-face
interactions for which there is no substitution.

Texting, although useful, may pose risks in addition to auto accidents! Like with over-involvement with computer activity,
excessive texting (for hours a day) may lead to focus problems
and pre-dispose youth to high-risk behaviors or problems like
absenteeism from school and fights. We don't know whether texting *caused* these problems or whether those with these
problems were texting more than others, but it does not hurt to
keep these concerns in mind.

Here are two real stories about how the Internet changed lives and relationships.

Jenna and **Paul** were friends for years. One day, out of the blue, Paul sent Jenna a graphic sexual message and pornographic photos through what he described as his "new online identity." Jenna was deeply shaken by this and did not respond. She had no idea what was behind his profound lapse in judgment, but however she looked at it, it was deeply disturbing. Was he on drugs when he sent it, or did the message "unmask" the "real" guy that she had not seen before? Was this the beginning of a stalking situation? What should she do? What had been a comfortable relationship became fearful and irreversibly damaged by mistrust.

Dana and **Travis** dated throughout high school and college, posting updates and photos of themselves and friends on their social network walls, which they made public to their online "friends." One day, when Dana was reading Travis' latest wall posting, she found a photo of him at a party with his arm around an unknown girl. Dana tagged the photo and got the girl's name (Jessica) and the names of her college, her high school, and even her high school prom date. This led to an angry confrontation between Dana and Travis, and they eventually broke up.

That was only the beginning of Dana's problems. She learned that other girls were trying to find out about her by tagging her photos posted on Travis' wall. Jessica used one of these photos to set up a fake account and post untrue information about Dana as well as private and embarrassing photos of her from the past. When anyone tagged a photo with Dana in it, a link was provided to this fake account. All of the false and private information became circulated among their online "friends." Worse, it was discovered by a potential employer, who had searched Dana's name through the major search engines and examined every-thing "public" on all of the popular social networking sites.

When Dana found out that Jessica had posted lies about her and posted private information and photos, she was upset and alarmed. She had already deleted former "friends" and changed her privacy settings in order to restrict access to her personal information and photos. But once the information had become "public," the cat was out of the bag, so to speak, and trying to undo the damage was exceedingly difficult. She had matured and hoped to put her past "mistakes" behind her, but the photos kept surfacing. As she confided to a friend, "I had to try to block every single connection I had made through my former boyfriend, but it was impossible, since I had no control over his 'friends' and their postings of photos of me." Although the breakup was two years ago, Dana is still trying to plug the holes in the system. And the potential employer? They decided to pass on Dana in favor of a less controversial applicant. Dana today is a wiser person—not yet free of regret and self-recrimination, but working on it, and still without a full-time job.

As Dana learned, some use social networking sites to *humiliate* or *harass*. These people are cowards, and the Internet has given them an easy and often risk-free way to feel powerful or relieve their boredom by inflicting pain on others, sometimes with fatal results. You may have heard about **Tyler Clementi**, the gay college student who took his own life after he was secretly filmed having sex with another man and the film was posted on the Internet. Or **Megan Meier**, the 13-year-old girl who hanged herself after being rejected by "Josh Evans," a fake online personality that had been constructed by the mother of a former friend reportedly to hurt Megan in retaliation for Megan's allegedly spreading gossip about the friend. When we talk later about the Shadow and the acting out of rage, we can see the psychological roots of these senseless acts of Internet-related violence.

In addition, some people use these resources for *illegal* purposes. Everyone knows that hackers want to invade our personal email and social networking accounts to steal our identities and money. Their communications are manipulative; they are seeking our usernames and pass codes or personal life details that might give clues to these. Even those useful online local classified sites can have their problems, as one buyer found when he agreed to come over to the seller's apartment with cash to buy and ended up being mugged and robbed.

Then there are people who are basically uncomfortable interacting face-to-face with others. For them, socializing will be a life-long struggle. The traditional mental health approach has been to support their taking small steps to connect to others, but many lack the confidence to do this. For many of these people, online relationships can be positive sources of *bridging capital* that they use to exchange information.

For others, cyber relationships are a *substitute* for real life ones. Some are seeking inappropriate or exploitative relationships and use social networking or other Internet sites to try to set these up. You have probably heard about cases in which pedophiles (adults who prefer to have sex with children or young teens) found their victims through the Internet, drawing them in by posing as a kid just a couple of years older. This may seem like an extreme example, but there are many cases of people having rude awakenings when they meet the "real person" behind the computer identity. One lonely young woman, a junior in college, was excited to meet a man she met online. When they arranged the meeting, he suddenly emailed her that he could not go through with it, because he was married. Bottom line: it can be difficult to penetrate the technological barriers in order to get to know the "real" person. When you applied to college, you provided teacher recommendations. When you apply for a job, you give references. In an online relationship, you have none of these helpful sources of information to help you check out this person. It is easy for Internet users to conceal what they don't want you to know and hide their true identities behind an anonymous username.

Finally, as the world becomes increasingly "connected," issues of *boundaries* and *privacy* loom large, as companies look to the Internet and social media to target advertising dollars to you and your "friends." Smart phones now have unique device identifiers that are inserted by the companies that carry the service or make the phones or operating systems. These identifiers can permit online tracking companies to gather data about you, including your age, sex, phone number, and in some cases, your geographical location, ethnicity, sexual orientation, and political views, and send this information to outside companies without your knowledge or permission. Interests and purchasing habits can be followed.

Most companies say that the sharing is anonymous and designed for "marketing" purposes, but it raises important questions. For example, you are walking down a street in Lafayette, Indiana. Over the past four years, you have purchased a number of computer games, so this interest is identified. As you walk along, ads for gaming stores appear on your smart phone, along with coupons for a discount at a local store that you just happen to be passing by. Or consider an application designed for exercisers. It has a motion detector that registers when you have completed your workout. Then it "rewards" you with ads and coupons for fitness drinks, energy bars, and vitamin waters.

It is also increasingly possible for smart phone providers to tap your publicly available information through the social networking sites you use. Advertisers know that if you are interested in computer games, your friends are likely to be as well, so similar alerts go out to them wherever they are.

Some see these trends as opening up exciting new opportunities to be an informed and smart consumer. And if these marketing pathways extend into areas of politics, religion, health concerns, and other major areas of our lives, they argue, so much the better. Others, however, see a relentless and escalating encroachment on our private lives and the lives of our friends and families. As one 18-year-old put it, "It is like having people knocking at your door 24/7. No boundaries and no peace!"

Some of these practices are being challenged legally, so how this issue of privacy will sort out in the future is unclear. However, the general principles remain. As in other major areas in your life, you will make decisions about how and when you will use the information and communication resources available through the Internet and social media. If you approach these decisions *consciously*, rather than *unconsciously*, keeping true to your values and the principles of moderation and balance, you can enjoy the benefits of this tremendous human invention while minimizing risks to your privacy, security, and health.

✗ Tools:

1. Be cautious about meeting people through the Internet. If you are participating in a group that shares a common interest, there is no need to tell them your real name or where you live, so don't.

2. Use judgment in sharing personal details on your wall post, such as your birth date, names of family members or pets, or other details that a hacker can use to steal your identity.

3. The same goes for any games or applications that you download into your computer or smart phone. Unless tracking devises become regulated or illegal for companies to install, be alert to them, and read the "licensing agreement" carefully before clicking to accept it.

4. When using social networking websites:

   A. Check into any available "opt out" options available from your smart phone provider to prevent transmission of information about you and your social network.

B. Avoid mentioning your exact location or stating that you will be out of town for a period of time in order to minimize the chance of a break-in where you live.

C. Looking for a job? Imagine a potential employer reading your postings, looking at your photos, and learning all about your romantic status. Before posting, think of grandma! If she would faint after viewing it, re-consider.

D. Check the settings "Friends Only" to make your profile and information Private.

E. Avoid accepting anyone in your network that you do not personally know.

5. Online dating services can be fine, but they can pose risks for both sexes. If you do use an online dating service, keep in mind (and these tips apply to both sexes unless otherwise specified):

A. Get to know the person slowly over a long time and have a number of phone conversations before you meet them in person.

B. Get your expectations out in the open. They may be expecting a lot more (or less) than you are. Better to know early and avoid disappointment later.

C. If you decide to meet the person, arrange to meet in a public place: Make it early, not late in the day, and limit it to a short period of time, like two hours, and don't forget your phone.

D. Women: find out about date rape testing strips, which are cards that you can take with you in your purse. These are a convenient way to test your drink for possible date rape drugs. (See Chapter 10, Sexuality, Tool #6). As an emergency precaution, take pepper spray and put it in your pocket where you can reach it easily. It is a good idea to take this with you whenever you are out late at night.

E. Go with a friend, who can meet the person and leave. If either of you gets a bad feeling about the person, arrange for a visual signal or verbal code that means you are uncomfortable and want to leave.

F. Inform several other friends where you are going, with whom, and when you expect to be home. Arrange to call a friend at a set time.

G. Do not let the new acquaintance bring you home. Take a cab or arrange a time and place to meet a friend who will walk or drive home with you. Make sure you are not followed.

H. Report any problems immediately to the authorities in your school and/ or community.

Lastly, keep online relationships in perspective. Remember that to be happy in life, you will need *real* relationships with real people, *not* just *virtual* relationships that live only in a computer. Can you imagine giving a dinner party for 450 of your "closest desktops" or reading this announcement about your friend: "Desiree Blank has become engaged to ThinkPad Number 4922208471"?

At the same time, develop a healthy relationship with technology, so that it does not fill your life with empty distractions that side-track you from the *"Prize"*! Only you can keep the Internet from taking over your life, stealing your time, and preventing you from enjoying the luxury of privacy and time to yourself. So turn off all of your communication devices and tell companies and others knocking at your virtual door 24/7 to come back when *you* want them to visit, not when *they* want to! Then get out, take a walk, and get with friends.

Protect your relationships from the technological forces that would harm them! When you are with your friends, make the most of these opportunities to deepen intimacy. *A machine is no substitute for the love and companionship of another human.*

- *Chapter Three* -

FINDING the FIT

Remember the story of Cinderella and how her mean step-sisters kept trying to squeeze their big feet into her tiny slipper? Of course, it failed in the end, because they just could not make that shoe fit, no matter how hard they tried. This is a great archetypal lesson about finding the life that fits. That shoe and the life that went with it belonged to Cinderella, not to them. Wouldn't it have been great if the stepsisters had told their mother to *"back off!"* while they went off in search of their own lives!

When we talked about identity in Chapter 1, we mentioned how, during the Transition, you will be looking for the roles you will play in adult life. In Chapter 2, we also talked about stepping out of the "collective unconscious" and finding the pathway that fits for you—the process Jung called "individuation." What you are seeking is the best "fit"—i.e. the roles in life that uniquely suit *you*, as you build your career and find a partner, friends, and interests. How do you know when you are there?

You are there when the mental, physical, spiritual, and emotional aspects of what you are doing combine to produce a *comfortable* and *satisfying* feeling. This signals that you have found your personal life *archetype*— a purposeful role in which you feel an emotional connection between your personal life and an ancient and universal human experience. Examples of these experiences, i.e., archetypes, include: *mother, father, sibling, friend, healer, counselor, warrior, teacher, leader, inventor,* and *helper.*

Some people find their archetype but reject it because it does not feel acceptable to them or their families. The following stories describe how two college students started going down paths that did not fit. Nick was influenced by his parents and the collective ideal of being a doctor, while Belinda was caught up in her college classmates' idea that "success" in life is measured by money. For Nick, change occurred after a vivid dream that connected to a powerful emotional archetypal. Belinda tried Wall Street for a while before stepping back and thinking about what she was doing. Both of them left the collective to find meaningful lives.

Nick, a 19 year-old college freshman, sought counseling for depression. He was taking pre-medical courses, having decided in high school that he wanted to be a physician. But as he began his second semester, he discovered that college level science and math courses were not as enjoyable as he had found those subjects to be in high school. The course he enjoyed most was philosophy, the only one on his schedule that was not pre-med. In his sophomore year, he began to have problems sleeping and concentrating. He found it difficult to muster the energy to do the work and even withdrew from his roommates and friends, who finally insisted that he go to the college health service for help. The health service physician suggested counseling.

Working with Nick, his counselor quickly sensed that he was on the wrong academic track. The son of Greek immigrants, he had chosen medicine because he wanted to please his parents. In high school, science classes were easy for him, so he did not question his choice. In college, however, the courses were harder and although he worked hard, he got only mediocre grades. He was putting in the effort but without much success. The counselor urged him to turn his attention to what he enjoyed in college. The only class he really liked was philosophy, which came easily to him. He realized that he had not enjoyed anything so much since being editor-in-chief of his high school newspaper.

He had the following dream. He was in medical school, dissecting a cadaver in anatomy class. The lab began to fill with water, but Nick was the only one drowning. He saw a boat on the distant horizon and began to swim to it. Socrates, the ancient Greek philosopher, was sitting inside, and helped him aboard. In the next dream, he and Socrates were sitting on the steps of the Parthenon talking.

Nick had an *archetypal* dream—a uniquely meaningful dream that makes us feel that we have tapped into ancient human wisdom. The dream helped him develop insight into the cause of his depression. As he worked through the meaning of the dream, he began to realize that medicine was not the right career for him. The dream also helped him to connect his Greek heritage with his high school passion for writing and his newly found interest and ability in philosophy. He changed his major to ancient Greek philosophy, eventually obtained a Ph.D., and has had a fulfilling career as a college professor.

When she was a senior in college, **Belinda** was among an elite group of students recruited to work for a prestigious bank in New York—the ideal job according to her classmates. She felt special to have been one of the lucky ones selected, but after she started working there, she found that the job required that she put in 18 hour days and engage in cut-throat competition for clients. She grew to hate coming in to work. Over the next year, she thought about what she really liked to do and realized that she had always enjoyed mentoring younger kids. When she had saved enough money, she left the job and entered graduate school to train to be a social worker, a career that she enjoys today. Thinking back to that first year out of college, she said, "Everyone in my class thought the ideal job was to be an investment banker making lots of money in New York. We were all caught up in the *thought* of it, but the *reality* was not the same. It was an *ugly ugly rat race!*"

✸ Tools:

1. Think about a role that seems to *fit* best with your personality, values, and life philosophy, including your mental, physical, spiritual, and emotional makeup (discussed further in the next chapter). This role will involve your life work or career, whether paid or unpaid, or a combination.

2. If you are struggling to figure out what career might fit, there are many online resources, including free online interest inventories. Here is only one of many available resources:

**http://www.career-test-info-guide.com/index.html
(click on "Take the Test")**

3. The "fit" may not be easy to find, and you might make a few false starts. That's okay. You can learn

from your mistakes and change course. Make the best choice you can given the knowledge you have at the time.

4. The "fit" may change over time! Keep a journal about your goals and any missteps along the way. Jot down dreams, episodes of synchronicity (see Chapter 9), and other experiences that seem to be important, even if you do not understand their meaning at the moment. These might lead you to the right pathway or even to your personal archetype.

5. Don't be discouraged by the redundant and sometimes monotonous aspects of any job you take. If you want to build loyalty, dependability, and credibility, the flat spots must be seen as part of the package. As we will discuss more in the next chapter, be careful about changing careers too often, as this can leave would be employers wary of your dependability.

6. It may be that because of circumstances, chance, and practical considerations, the life work you per-

form might not be the perfect fit but, rather, the best option available at hand. Think positively and value the contribution you are making! Every constructive role can benefit others and has its part to play in life.

- *Chapter Four* -

The BIG PICTURE

THE FOUR COMPASS POINTS OF LIFE–Mental, Physical, Spiritual, and Emotional

This is the time to think about the Big Picture and develop a philosophy that helps you live life and solve problems while keeping your emotions and actions in balance. This chapter will talk about one such philosophy. It is a simple concept of "*4 Compass Points of Life.*" Each day, think about how you will take care of the needs of each of these areas, and you will go far in achieving balance in your life. Neglecting any of them can lead to imbalance and possibly medical or emotional problems, but overdoing it in any one area can also cause problems, so strive for both *balance* and *moderation*. The compass points are:

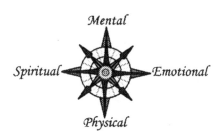

Mental

Spiritual — Emotional

Physical

The *Mental* compass point concerns the intellectual tasks of life—education or academic pursuits and, ultimately, our life's work, whether paid, unpaid, or a combination of both. Developing this part of ourselves is one of the two great challenges of adult life. Pay attention to school, and when you do take a job, do it to the best of your ability. Learn to be a reliable employee with a "can-do" attitude. Stay with it and don't impulsively quit without a very good reason. Even though the work you have at the moment may not be what you ultimately want to do, you are learning commitment and gaining valuable experience while you work on your career.

✗ *Tools:*

1. If you are in school and not enjoying a course of study, (like with Nick), can you talk with your advisor and make a change? Help is available. Seek it.

2. If you are working and don't like your job, take time to think about what the problem is. Does the job not suit your personality, interests, or abilities? Is the work environment or hours stressful? Do you feel inadequate to the task and in need of more training or education? Are your coworkers or bosses difficult? Are the circumstances (like a long commute) aggravating you? Weigh the pluses and minuses. If this job is the best option for now and you cannot easily change it, try to change your attitude. Difficulties teach us a lot about ourselves, and learning to manage problems helps us to grow. Here is an example of a young man who could not change the circumstances of his job, so he changed himself.

Desmond had an hour and a half commute in traffic each way to his internship. He found himself becoming progressively angrier and more frustrated with this waste of time until he realized that he had to come to grips with the situation. He could not change things, so he thought of ways to adapt. He listened to music, audio books, or used the time to think about problems and life in general. Soon, the dreaded commute became his special alone time.

3. Every career and job has its ups and downs. Emphasize the strong points and try not to dwell on the deficiencies. Before you quit, have a practical plan in mind to improve your career situation or get some career counseling.

4. If you are not quitting in order to return to school, don't quit without having secured a new job. Try not to be someone who changes jobs frequently, as such a pattern often raises red flags in the minds of future employers.

5. If you make a mistake, it's not the end of the world! You have just "bought some experience." You can course correct, like Nick and Belinda did.

6. If the only rub is money, ask yourself some hard questions. Are your expectations realistic and fair? Are you making enough to live? Can your employer afford to pay you more? Does this job reward you in

other ways that you would lose if you left— like giving you coworkers that are friends, or work that is, by its nature, helpful to others?

7. Some young people, like Belinda, get caught up in a money-driven "rat race" and can't seem to get out of it. Are you? This is a slippery slope, with major implications for your mental and physical health, relationships, and your soul. Read about the Money Shadow below (page 89).

The *Physical* compass point concerns our bodies. Physical health promotes a sense of well-being. Develop life-long habits to take care of your health. Learn to eat moderately but wisely and avoid harmful substances. Be active and get some exercise on a daily basis— take walks, play a sport, or work out on machines at the gym. No time? You can build in exercise by taking the stairs rather than elevators or getting a parking place that gives you a little hike.

Get regular medical checkups and pay attention to symptoms that may need medical attention. If you are unsure if a symptom is serious or not, it will not hurt to have it checked out. It may save your life as occurred with the following young man, in whose life I happened to intervene:

At the age of 25, **John** started having unusual headaches that he had never had before. When his girlfriend mentioned it to me, I suggested he see his regular doctor and arrange to get a CT scan of his head. He did, and the scan revealed a type of aneurysm, or ballooning out of an artery. This is a rare condition that is often not diagnosed before it suddenly ruptures and results in death. This young man was lucky. Paying attention to his headaches rather than ignoring them led to an evaluation, diagnosis, and an uncomplicated surgery that saved his life.

⚒ Tools:

1. As you care for yourself, tune in to your circadian rhythms. Biorhythm theory states that our mental, physical, emotional energies run on separate cycles. For both sexes, the physical is 23 days; the emotional, 28 days, and the intellectual, 33 days. Sometimes you may notice a synergy that leaves you feeling strong and energetic in all areas. This happens when all three cycles peak together in a "triple critical high." Take advantage of these moments! Other times you may feel profoundly fatigued in all domains and cannot seem to accomplish much of anything. At that time, if we are not ill, the three systems may have con-

verged in a "triple critical low." Most of the time we live in between these extremes.

2. Learn what works for your body and do an honest inventory. Ask yourself questions like how much sleep do you really need to function? Are you a morning or evening person? What foods keep your blood sugar stable and don't cause you to gain (or lose) too much weight? How much exercise can you reasonably do consistently? You have one body to use your whole life. Take care of it.

The **Spiritual** Compass Point helps us grapple with the ultimate questions of life and our place within it. It is also the basis for the *ethical code* that will guide our actions. Ethics involve both what you *do* and what you *refrain from doing*. Humans have always struggled with these questions, but the Internet has created all new challenges for age-old ethical issues, like being honest and not harming others. How would you handle these two real situations?

Nelson, a high school senior, downloaded a paper from the Internet and turned it in as his own. His classmates knew about this, but no one said anything, and the teacher never found out. He was accepted into an elite college.

Rosa, who was temporarily mad at her friend, **Amber**, violated a confidence by mentioning on Facebook that Amber's father had gone to prison—a fact that Amber, who was deeply ashamed, did not want to reveal. The public posting of this private hurt so devastated Amber that she became physically ill and dropped out of school, because she could not face her classmates. She was so ashamed that later, she transferred to a different school, where slowly she made new friends. Rosa felt very remorseful about having broken her word, but the relationship was, unfortunately, beyond repair.

Perhaps you have already established a spiritual base and a strong sense of ethics, or you may be so busy that you don't even think about this compass point at all. Maybe this is a part of you that will need to develop and grow over time. If the Spiritual Compass Point is not a high priority right now, keep these tools in your back pocket for later.

Tools:

1. Spiritual awareness is a gift given only to humans among all living things. A strong spiritual life gives comfort and stability to life and helps us get through traumatic events and stress that otherwise we might not endure. It also gives hope, both for this life and beyond.

2. Without the spiritual element, life can devolve into meaningless existence without a feeling of higher purpose or any goal other than one's own personal survival or gain. On your journey, keep asking yourself, "What is my purpose here? What am I supposed to do with my life? What is the **Prize**?"

3. Many turn to the great religions of the world, seeking help from a Higher Power or God to resolve problems, gain comfort, and provide the principles for living life in harmony with others. Others seek answers from philosophy, which seeks to understand the meaning of life, or psychology, which studies behavior and emotions. Find a framework that works for you. You will need it sooner or later.

4. Ethics come from a spiritual grounding. Form an ethical code that infuses all your relationships and activities. Here are a few ideas:

A. The "Golden Rule" does not mean "He who has the Gold makes the Rules!" It is a timeless principle that urges us to treat others as we want to be treated.

69

B. Keep your word.

C. Practice tolerance as a part of your code of life. There are many ways to "skin the cat," and not everyone needs to choose the same one. Although others may skin it in a way that is irritating to you, your way may annoy them too. Everyone has good and bad qualities. It may be hard to see the good in others for their flaws, but if you can develop tolerance, you can diminish unnecessary emotional distress. A wise man said, "Everyone has something like a computer chip from God." Even if the man could not see the "chip" in others, he knew that it was there. This knowledge enabled him to accept people who behaved in difficult ways.

D. Use it or lose it applies to ethics along with everything else in life! If you don't live by your ethical code and the principles it contains, it is meaningless.

The *Emotional* Compass Point is such a large and important topic that the entire next chapter is devoted to it.

- *Chapter Five* -

The EMOTIONAL COMPASS POINT

THE SOUL AND THE EMOTIONS— Happiness and Pain

You are in a period of life in which emotions run high. It is not uncommon to have feelings of sadness, anxiety, anger, shame, jealousy, sexual arousal, and confusion. Most women do have highs and lows depending on their periods. Guys can struggle with feeling keyed up sexually. Situations and people will evoke strong emotional reactions that make us act in ways that can either help our lives or create problems and unhappiness for us and others. How can we manage the powerful emotions that flood us on a daily basis?

THE PSYCHOLOGICAL TASKS OF LIFE

"What is life really about and what is the point of it all?" Or to ask the question another way, what is the *"Prize"* here? Where do we hope to be when we come out of the next few years, and the lifetime after that?

Basing his work on Freud, psychologist Erik Erikson concluded that the two major tasks of adult life are to *love* and to *work*. Becoming that person is not easy, because it involves getting in touch with our emotions, most of which reside outside of our awareness and lie instead in the unconscious, in urges and desires that can govern our behavior in powerful ways.

Gaining awareness or insight into our emotions and what is triggering them can give us more power to make choices about how we react and behave. The more we understand about our emotions, the more we can choose actions that further happiness rather than distress.

THE CONSCIOUS AND THE UNCONSCIOUS

There are two major emotional arenas — the conscious and the unconscious. We already discussed the "collective unconscious," but in addition, we have an individual unconscious, where most of the emotions that govern our lives reside. In this vast murky ocean are the two most powerful unconscious forces—the *sexual* and the *aggressive* drives, according to Freud.

Human society has rules about sexual and aggressive behavior, and it imposes social and legal consequences for violations of that code. Individuals, too, have ethics that keep those drives under control. External rules and internal self-discipline are meant to keep us from committing destructive acts that will harm ourselves or others and cause us guilt and pain. But sometimes those urges seem to take on a life of their own, causing us to take leave of our senses and throw good judgment out the window. In the midst of a storm of emotions, we can behave in ways that are aberrant for us, like when Rosa posted Amber's private hurt on Facebook.

The aberration need not be destructive, just different. You may notice such a change when you fall in love—something that we will discuss below. You are attracted to someone and find yourself acting in unusual ways around them. Or you may notice a change in someone else, as when a friend suddenly starts ignoring you or behaving in a hostile or overly critical way. When these things are happening to you or others, it means that we have lost control of those powerful unconscious drives—sexual, aggressive, or both. Those forces are managing us, rather than the other way around. So the question is: if the drives reside in the unconscious, how can we make them known to the conscious mind? How can we recognize and manage them, so that we can avoid trouble?

✗ Tools:

1. Learn to connect physical sensations and emotional states through relaxation techniques and "body scanning." Develop a sense of your physical reactions to intense emotion — how anger and other strong feelings such as attraction, shame, sadness, fear, and anxiety feel in your body. Search "Emotional Intelligence" on the Internet to learn more about this idea.

2. You can learn a lot about yourself through accidental slips of the tongue, which Freud called "parapraxis". Here are some examples:

Rich had just met **Janine** in class and was immediately attracted to her. Afterward, he asked if she wanted to get together for coffee. Janine agreed, asking, "When do you have time?" Rich began thumbing through his schedule, stating, "How about Friday—my schedule has been so *erotic* lately!" They both laughed. Rich's unconscious sexual feelings

74

had slipped out from his unconscious into his speech.

A doctor treating an anorexic woman wrote a chart note saying that the patient was having trouble with her *edible complex.*

3. Here is something to think about—your dreams! They give us messages directly from the source—the unconscious. If you have a dream that feels important when you wake up, it probably is. It can tell you how you really feel about a situation or a person, even though you may not realize these feelings in your waking life. The following story shows how dreams helped one young woman solve a big problem:

Alexis, age 26, had been working in investments in New York for five years. For the first four years she was with one company, but was then laid off in a down-sizing. The next year, she worked for a smaller company that was trying to establish itself as a major player in the field. When she took the job, she thought that there would be a team approach and she would have ample resources to help her do her work effectively. But this turned out not to be the case, and after a year, reluctantly, she began to answer calls from recruiters about other jobs. Months went by, and the situation at work deteriorated, but Alexis had mixed feelings about what to do. She expressed her concerns directly to her boss. Rather than listen, he patted her on the back and told her to "lighten up" while he worked on his computer. She did not want to be a quitter, but despite her best efforts, she couldn't find a solution to the problems at work.

One night she had the following dream: Her boss and coworkers were sky-diving from the top of the office building, while Alexis remained at her desk answering calls and frantically trying to cover everyone's clients. She felt anger and anxiety about the situation—anger toward the others who were engaged in a reckless activity rather than doing their jobs, and anxiety about their safety and her own inability to do everyone's work adequately. The dream clarified Alexis's feelings about her situation by showing with absolute clarity her deepest unconscious feelings about the workplace. This resolved her uncertainty and helped her to decide to take another job. Meanwhile, the boss's denial of problems, inability to listen, and poor communication skills cost him a good employee while fostering a demoralized, out of control work environment.

What do you do in your personal life when somebody "acts out" in a way that betrays you and hurts your friendship? A friend or acquaintance is doing things that make you feel angry, like lashing out or avoiding you, or maybe you see your friend getting into destructive activities or relationships without a thought about the consequences. The person seems to be in the grip of emotions and unaware or unreasoning about the true nature of his or her actions. Here is an example of how strong unconscious anger harmed a relationship:

Dawn and **Jackie** had become fast friends since entering college a few months ago. Things were great until Jackie started dating Sam. Dawn suddenly became withdrawn and cool toward Jackie.

When Jackie asked what was wrong, Dawn lashed out in a hostile attack. Devastated, Jackie told a friend what had happened. The friend told her that Dawn had wanted to date Sam and was jealous and angry that he was dating Jackie. Although Jackie tried to maintain the friendship, Dawn continued her hostile behavior, denied problems, and refused to communicate about what was going on. Eventually, their relationship dissolved.

Here, jealousy overtook Dawn and caused her to act out in a hostile and aggressive way toward Jackie, who could not "right" the relationship, no matter how much she tried. For things to have changed, Dawn would have had to recognize her anger as unfair and be willing to make amends. As well as apologizing to Jackie, Dawn would also have to work on her own feeling of jealousy and the disappointment that lay beneath it. This is very difficult for all of us to do. It takes a great deal of wisdom and self-control. More often, people tend to make small gestures toward reconciliation, with the big problem never being directly discussed. Sometimes, with these half-measures, relationships can get somewhat patched up. However, some relationships are never repaired, because the unresolved emotions remain too strong.

What can you do when anger is escalating in your relationship?

⚒ Tools:

1. Communicating is essential— but do so at a time when you feel in control of your own feelings. How to cool off before this conversation? A good, sweaty workout can take the edge off of the anger and relax you. Meditation may also help you to become calm and focused. Make a list of points you want to make and give some specific examples of what the person is doing that has upset you.

2. Use good communication tools. Begin your thoughts with "I" statements, like "I feel that our relationship has been distant lately." This can soften the approach, so that the other person is less likely to feel personally attacked. Even if it is the other person that is acting out, take responsibility for your own feelings but allow for the possibility that you are mistaken: "I have felt hurt by your behavior but maybe I am misunderstanding something?" This can defuse tensions and allow the other person to meet you halfway. Once you have communicated your feelings, *stop* and *listen* to what they have to say.

3. If you recognize that your emotions are controlling you and disrupting your relationships, talking to a friend or a counselor can help. Sharing feelings can give us a better perspective on them; a sympathetic listener makes it easier for us to get in touch with our feelings by making it safe for us to talk about them. In this process, our unconscious feelings become more conscious, and that makes it possible to solve our problems using good judgment.

4. What if you are not involved but are worried about your friend, who is head over heels in love with someone who is treating him or her badly. You think that the relationship is destructive, and you want to say something. Here, use caution! Remember that you are viewing the situation from the standpoint of an outsider. You may or may not be right, but whatever the truth happens to be, your friend will have to discover it for himself or herself. Just let them know that you are there for them as a friend.

5. What if your friend is getting into destructive activities, like alcohol, drugs, bingeing, or starving.

Express your concerns directly as a friend, using "I" statements and examples of what you have seen. Here is an example, "I am concerned about you! I have seen you drunk every day this past week, and I am worried about your health!" See Chapter 10 for more information on problems, and share the resources with your friend.

THE ROLE OF THE DEFENSE MECHANISMS

"Gee, you don't have to be so _defensive!_" Has anyone said that to you? If so, someone probably "pushed your buttons," and you let them know! The "buttons" are our psychological defense mechanisms. They signal a threat and trigger a response that is meant to protect us and decrease our immediate anxiety or fear. Everyone has defense mechanisms. Without them, we would not be able to cope with life. But, as with nearly everything else, there is a downside. If we are prickly and defensive all the time because people are pushing our buttons, people will have a hard time relating to us at all, much less getting close. Plus, being defensive all the time consumes a lot of emotional energy. So, if you can learn to deactivate these buttons, it can reduce stress. Here are three of the most common defense mechanisms:

Repression is simply forgetting something that is unpleasant or uncomfortable to think about. We can think of repression as a way to "metabolize" the stress of everyday life. Without some way to keep painful or unpleasant occurrences from dominating our awareness, we would not be able to function. Think about the scary or unpleasant things you dealt with as a small child—receiving an injection from a nurse, going to the dentist, getting your first haircut, waking up from a frightening dream, or being hurt in an accident. Remember how worrying or thinking about those things made it difficult to think about anything else?

A *memory lapse* can be an example of repression. Not remembering an appointment may tell us that unconsciously, we did not want to go. What about forgetting an assignment in school or neglecting to bring home a book? We may not be aware of it, but maybe we felt negatively about the assignment, the subject, or school. Pay attention to such lapses, because they can have significant consequences. If you "forgot" to bring that paper to school, you may get an F!

Denial helps us manage something that feels overwhelming. Soldiers who are on a dangerous combat mission must focus entirely on what they have to do and don't let themselves think about being killed. Emotionally, they *deny* the immediate danger in order to carry out their mission. Remember Jackie and Dawn? Dawn denied that there were any problems as a way of dealing with her anger and jealousy. Even people who are dying from a terminal illness may deny that there is anything wrong with them. Very commonly, denial protects us from painful feelings like *shame*, which we will talk about later. Alexis' boss did not have the skills necessary to correct the work environment and address her valid concerns, which raised for him deeper feelings of shame, inadequacy, and fears of humiliation and failure. As a result, he just denied that there were real problems but made it seem like Alexis was the issue and needed to "lighten up."

Projection involves attributing to others a feeling that actually comes from inside us. One man who was insecure about being gay thought everyone around him was making fun of him, while another man, who was full of anger, believed that everyone was out to get him. These are extreme examples of a defense mechanism that we all use. Projection can leave us feeling mistrustful, angry, or fearful of others, and it can be hard to recognize that the feeling is coming from *us* rather than *them*. Learn how this feels physically, especially in the pit of your stomach, and do a reality check to see how much of your feeling is coming from *inside*, rather than *outside*.

What happened between Jackie and Dawn also illustrates projection at work. When Jackie tried to explain her hurt feelings, Dawn lashed out at Jackie for attacking her. In truth, it was Dawn who attacked Jackie, but now she was attributing,

83

or *projecting,* her own hostility and anger onto Jackie. At first Jackie questioned herself, thinking that she must have done something wrong. Feeling herself spinning under a cloud of confusion and depression, Jackie sought some help. A few counseling sessions helped her to understand more clearly the dynamics between the two. This bit of "preventive medicine" helped Jackie avoid defending herself by lashing out in retaliation toward Dawn—a "no-win" situation. Instead, Jackie broadened her circle of friends and decreased her expectations of Dawn, leaving Dawn to deal with her own problems. Jackie learned to distance herself from Dawn's anger and avoid getting entangled in it. This helped her avoid making a bad situation worse by responding in kind. Below, there are more specific tools to help in these situations.

ENCOUNTER WITH THE SHADOW—Projecting the Negative

Here is a personal story. At 17, I left Alabama to attend college in the East, excited to join what I thought was an ideal environment of freedom, tolerance, and academic enlightenment. At that time in the 1960s, George Wallace, Governor of Alabama and candidate for President, was often in the news because of his anti-civil rights and segregationist views. To say the least it was a controversial time to be an Alabama native in a hyper-liberal college. A couple of weeks into freshman year, I returned to my room one night only to

84

find tomatoes and eggs splattered all over my door along with anti-South graffiti. My friends explained that a highly intoxicated upperclassman, **Jane**, and her friends had camped outside my door and defaced it while shouting, "Come out, you *George Wallace Lover, you!*" Jane was a New Yorker studying Marxist political philosophy. I shrugged off the incident and went on.

The next year, Jane asked to meet with me privately. She produced a rose and asked, "Can you ever forgive me for what I did to you?" Surprised, I replied, "I forgave you long ago," (which was true). "Besides," I said, "you learned something about me, I learned something about you." She is now a civil rights attorney in New York.

For years, as the incident passed across my mind, I wondered, "What was *that* all about?" Later, during my psychiatric residency program, I learned that it was about the *Shadow*— the negative human traits that we abhor in ourselves and project onto others rather than recognize and work with them within our own lives. Jane had projected her Shadow onto me. She had never met me and knew nothing about me, including my racial views, but the fact that I was from Alabama had struck a cord within her, evoking Shadow qualities that were psychologically "carried" by George Wallace— prejudice, racism, conservatism, and ignorance. Under the influence of alcohol, Jane's normal inhibitions were gone, and the unconscious Shadow contents of her mind had emptied onto my door that night.

As Jane learned, projection of negative or "Shadow" qualities can cause trouble for us and for others and can require us to "undo" damage later on. Just like we cannot get rid of our shadow on a sunny day, we cannot get rid of our psychological Shadow. What are the Shadow qualities that you find distasteful in others? Think of people you really dislike. What qualities do they exhibit? Greed, arrogance, irresponsibility, naïveté, authoritarianism, seductiveness, hostility, bigotry, passivity, snobbishness, dishonesty, entitlement? Maybe these are your Shadow qualities. It is hard to accept them as being part of ourselves; much easier to deny them and project them onto others, but if you "own" them, you can work on them.

✗Tools:

1. To get a handle on the Shadow, first learn to monitor your emotional reactions to people or situations. Recognize the negative emotions that are being triggered. Fear? Anxiety? Anger?

2. If it is anger, here is good advice from Thomas Jefferson: "When angry, count ten before you speak; if very angry, count a hundred."

3. If you are reacting intensely and negatively to a person or situation, think of what you learned in elementary school about how to look out for traffic when crossing the street: *Stop, Look, and Listen*. Stop the emotional over-reaction. Look at the meaning the person or situation has for you. Listen to what your inner wisdom has to say about it. Writing your thoughts and dreams in a journal or talking to someone may help tone down your feelings.

4. Try for a moderate response. Think of your feelings on a scale of -10 to +10, with zero being "neutral," -10 being "too negative," and +10 being "too positive." This is the **Emotions Scale:**

-10 _____ 0 _____ +10
(Too Negative!)   (Balanced)   (Too Positive!)

Try to stay around 0 as much as you can. If you are angry, you are in the negative zone on your emotional scale. Learn to wait before responding. Time can often soften our reactions and give us perspective.

5. Consider whether it is "they" who are making you uncomfortable, or if it is what they represent that may be posing the problem. Like I was for Jane, the person may be a Shadow figure for you— representing attitudes and ideas that are in conflict with your ideals.

6. If the person is a Shadow figure for you, stop and think about the encounter rather than act out

your anger. See it as an opportunity to learn about yourself. Work on taking back the projection. The person who evoked these feelings is neither all good nor all bad but probably a blend of the two, as all people are.

7. If it is someone you have just met, take a chance, set aside that initial reaction, and talk to the person. Get to know him or her better. Sometimes a quickly formed opinion of someone completely changes with more knowledge. You have probably had the experience of thinking that someone was pretty awful and then finding out that he or she was not so bad after all. The negativity became neutralized, and you discovered some positive qualities that you had not seen the first time around. If we see both the positives and negatives of a person, we are probably seeing him or her realistically.

A Word about the "Money Shadow"

In our society, money has become much more than a medium of exchange for the necessities of life. It is loaded with meaning about self-worth, position, and power. For some, the acquisition of money means escape from past poverty and misery and the ability to lead or to offer to children a better life than they had when they were growing up. Others with altruistic goals view money as a way to help others, like friends, family, institutions, or the community.

Like other aspects of life, money has a Shadow side, which has to do with power and the ability to manipulate, control, or dominate others. The Money Shadow, like the other Shadow qualities, is in everyone. You have probably seen people whose lives are dominated by the Money Shadow and whose relationships, family, and community suffer as a result. Like Belinda learned, in their careers, some people get themselves into a competitive "race to wealth" that may involve others or just themselves. There is no winning this race, because for them, there is never enough money.

Sometimes the Money Shadow can bring about financial ruin, as people acquire things they cannot afford in order to impress others. Politicians and celebrities lose careers and families because of money-related ethical violations. Even worse, however, is the diminishing effect the Money Shadow can have on our values and character. Sometimes it is frugality to the point of stinginess that takes the fun and joy out of life. Sometimes it is reckless spending, gambling, or ethically questionable activities that lead to bankruptcy or legal problems. In plain terms, the Money Shadow is about greed. The struggle against its destructive nature is a timeless theme in literature and the arts, as seen in Richard Wagner's operas, the *Ring Cycle*, and J.R.R. Tolkien's trilogy, *Lord of the Rings*. But here's the paradox: beneath the greed are feelings of emptiness and loss. Unless these are dealt with emotionally, money will maintain its death-grip on our lives.

✗ Tools:

1. Cultivate a healthy relationship with money. Use it wisely, but don't allow it to control your life, career, relationships, or self-esteem.

2. Hold to your own values and standards rather than using wealth to measure your self-worth or the worth of others.

3. Help others, but avoid being manipulated to support their destructive behaviors, either financially or emotionally.

4. Be generous in appropriate circumstances. Altruism is among the most noble of human qualities, enriching our lives in a way that nothing else can.

FALLING IN LOVE—Projecting the Ideal

If we can project our *Shadow* side onto others, we can also project its opposite— our *Idealized Self*. You may recognize that this happens when you meet someone that you instantly like or admire. You engage in lively conversation, exchange information, and eagerly anticipate getting together again. The person seems to embody all of the qualities you admire. You become friends or even fall in love.

Now we enter the *honeymoon phase* of a relationship, and it feels great! We think that it will last forever, and we don't want to lose the way we feel when we are with or think about the other person. Sexual feelings may be strong, whether or not we are aware of them. Our world is wonderful and beautiful — until something happens to break the spell. Maybe you discover something that disappoints you. Or maybe you learn, painfully, that you are disappointing the other person or that your feelings are not reciprocated, at least not with the intensity that you feel them. The two of you no longer meet each other's expectations.

You may discover differences on important issues, or there may be tensions about trivial irritations, like when one person is constantly texting, while the other one is trying to discuss something. There may be control battles over time, as one young woman found when she dated a guy who was never available for the agreed-upon date until late at night after all of the post-game parties were over. Or money gets to be an issue, with arguments over who picks up the costs of going out. You both try to work things out, but the other person is no longer the "perfect" friend or lover you imagined you had found. Perhaps the friendship will survive, but it may not be as meaningful or rewarding as it was, or the relationship may end, amicably and with mutual regret, or with anger and disappointment. In any of these cases you ask yourself, *"What happened?"*

When we fall in love, we project our Idealized Selves onto another person. The process of projection is the same as when we project our Shadow side, but the emotions are different. In one case we feel anger and fear; in the other, we feel enraptured, elated, and energized. Here is a good example of what happens when we fall in love.

Ellen met **Tom** on the first day of class. Tall, slender, with penetrating blue eyes, he smiled at her and introduced himself. In that first conversation, they talked and joked about the class. From then on, they started to see a lot of each other. For Ellen, Tom was perfect. He was the funniest, best looking, and brightest guy she had ever known. He had a charisma and charm that drew everyone (including other girls) to him. They talked about everything, and he seemed to care about her. Their dates seemed to go well, and gradually they got physically involved, which, for Ellen, was sensational. She was in love and thought he was too. She found herself waiting for Tom to call and canceling other plans in order to go out with him. Her girl friends started getting upset and angry about the way she put her whole life on hold for Tom, but Ellen explained that Tom's busy schedule sometimes required last minute changes.

Over time, his calls became less and less frequent. Suddenly he stopped calling her altogether and made it a point to avoid her in class. She was devastated and confused. She confronted him and asked to talk. He was obviously uncomfortable and talked about how he did not want to make any commitments at this point in his life. He mentioned that his parents were divorced, and he did not want to make the same mistakes that they had. He said that he "thought" she was the girl he wanted to end up with, but he wanted to "take it slowly" and remain friends for the time being. Ellen was hurt but responded with all the patience and understanding she could muster. For months she clung to the hope that he would "come back around," but he never did. When she saw him walking across campus with another girl, she realized that she had been dumped. It took a long time to recover from this disappointment.

Jesse fell in love with **Nora**, and they quickly became involved. She was his "ideal woman," until once, at a party, she became drunk and ended up in bed with another guy. When Jesse confronted her, she screamed back, "You're the problem, not me! I can do what I want, and you have no right to control me!" Jesse was shocked and furious, later realizing that he had seriously misjudged her character. Like Ellen had done with Tom, Jesse, at first, could see only Nora's positive traits-- his internal idea of perfection, which he had projected onto her. Later, when the projection dropped away, he was left with only the real, rather than fantasy woman, who turned out not to be a good fit for him after all.

When people are in love they usually see only perfection in the other person. But perfection is not a natural state. When we idealize someone, inevitably our perception will sooner or later give way to the realities of an imperfect world and human flaws. This person is not perfect, and neither are you. Both of you have flaws. Are the problems you discover ones that you can accept and live with? Or — like habits of alcohol or drugs, gambling, infidelity — do they feel emotionally insurmountable for you?

What remains after the projections fall away? How can you trust your feelings, and what is "true love?" Love is based first on friendship, and a true friend is someone who has a deep and abiding interest in you. Such genuine concern for another person forms the foundation for mature love. Love happens when you know and accept the good and bad qualities of another person, and the other person also accepts you uncritically. This will be someone who wears well in the long run, a person who can communicate when there is a problem, rather than avoid or act out destructively when angry or upset — someone who can recognize his or her part in the problem, rather than unfairly place all the blame on you, leaving you feeling guilty or bad about yourself while they disavow any responsibility.

What if you are acting on those principles yourself, but the other person is not? You are valuing the relationship— showing interest, communicating when problems arise, and recognizing your role in problems—but instead of meeting you halfway, as with Jesse and Nora, the response is denial, avoidance, betrayal, criticism or other hurtful actions. Stop and take another look at the relationship. It may be time for a change.

✄ Tools:

1. Remember the **Emotions Scale (p. 88)?** Maybe you have gone too far in the positive direction. Ask yourself some hard questions. Have you overlooked or rationalized behaviors that did not match the "perfect" image you had of someone? Has the person become unreliable? Do you give higher priority to the other person's needs and feelings than he or she gives to yours? If you don't do your own reality check, it may be done for you when the other person breaks off the relationship. This hurts and it may hurt for a long time to come. But "this, too, shall

pass" is true. Give yourself time and seek the support of friends who can tide you over this bad time. You will heal and find the right person for you.

2. Are you in an abusive relationship? You should not tolerate this. Go to:

www.loveisrespect.org

Or call the National Teen Dating Abuse Helpline at **866-331-9474 (TTY: 866-331-8453)**. People are there to help you. You deserve a good relationship.

3. If your feelings plunge to an extreme depth and you feel worthless, hopeless, and alone, you may be plunging into an abyss of blackness, i.e. clinical depression. Talk to family, a proven friend, or a counselor. The important thing is to get help, so that you can get perspective, heal the hurt, and move on.

4. If your love relationship ends, do not give up. And above all, don't think that you will never love again. You have gained wisdom and have a better sense of what you need.

5. Learn to communicate about problems. Try not to let the sun set on your anger. Remember that the word *danger* has *anger* in it. If you cannot communicate with someone, the relationship will not make it.

6. If your boyfriend or girlfriend says, "You are making me unhappy," don't buy it. We cannot *make* others unhappy or happy, just like they cannot *make* us feel these emotions either. Each of us has to do that for ourselves.

7. Keep focused on your life goals while you try out different relationships. Sometimes it takes years to find the right fit. If you find that special person, be grateful and cherish the relationship. Remember:

"Choose Your Love and Love your Choice!"

8. If you feel like you are really trying but failing to accomplish your goal of finding a partner, do a reality check with a friend or a counselor. Are you being too picky? Are you choosing the wrong types of people?

Are you so independent that it is hard to compromise? Or are you overly dependent— giving up too much of yourself for someone else? While you are sorting out these questions, keep living. We all have to get comfortable with ourselves as individuals, whether a partner is there or not. Make a family of friends — people who will walk down the road of life with you. A true friend, one who shares our interests and values and cares about us, is one of life's greatest gifts.

REALITY CHECK— Difficult People and How They Act

We learned above that denial and projection are the least adaptive of our defenses, because *they do not deal effectively with reality*. We are not seeing others realistically and therefore are reacting to them based on distorted perceptions. But sometimes our negative reactions are completely accurate and represent reality, not something we imagined or exaggerated. There are people who are truly difficult.

Zoë was a brilliant and beautiful young woman with a soprano voice that had helped her to be admitted to an elite college. **Pat**, one of her four roommates, was in awe of Zoë, whom she constantly tried to please. Zoë generally reacted with indifference, but she could attack with a vengeance if she did not get her way. The roommates did not appreciate her sense of entitlement, for example, her race to be the first in the shower each morning and her endless excuses for not doing her share of the cleaning. Zoë's idea of compromise was for the roommates to give in, which they mostly did, after many heated confrontations brought no change.

Pat tried to smooth out tensions between the roommates. But the more Pat tried to be Zoë's friend, the more aloof and critical Zoë became. Finally, in tears, Pat had a long talk with one of her friends, asking, "What's wrong with me?" The friend responded, "Nothing. Zoë treats everyone the same way. She is an *equal opportunity jerk*." Eventually, to everyone's relief, Zoë transferred to a single room. A stormy relationship with a boyfriend finally broke up, as he discovered that beneath the pretty exterior was a person who was fundamentally selfish and self-centered.

Tony was a star quarterback in high school and found himself recruited by a number of prestigious schools. He was a truly gifted athlete, and he knew it. Modesty was not in his vocabulary. He did not walk; he swaggered. He was the best and enjoyed the attention this designation gave him. Senior year in high school was quite a year. He was flown to various colleges and "wined and dined" by the coaches. When interviewed by admissions officers, his demeanor was, "You should be so lucky to get me." The irksome thing was that he seemed to get away with it. The scholarship offers came rolling in, and he took his pick.

Zoë and Tony *really* were difficult people; this was no *illusion*. Human beings come with all kinds of personalities, some easier, some harder to deal with. Most people have a mix of different traits, many of which may already be entrenched by late adolescence. Usually we should try to take people as they are, get to know them, work with their strengths, and negotiate the weaknesses. In some instances, however, one element can dominate and cause problems. **Obsessive compulsives** can be rigid and controlling, while **histrionics** tend to be "fickle," dramatic, and impulsive. For Zoë and Tony, excessive **narcissism** was coloring their behavior, giving them hard edges that repelled others. So far they seemed to have suffered no negative consequences from their style, and maybe they will never change. But they are young and have not yet encountered any major stumbling blocks. Rejection, failure, and disappointment can be strong motivators of change. Life may yet present them the opportunity to soften the traits that are already interfering with their relationships.

Occasionally we run up against someone who is *exceptionally difficult*. Nature is imperfect, and there are people who have significant character defects that do not change much, if at all, in life. Sometimes, pathological narcissists fit into this category, but the ultimate character-flawed type is the antisocial personality (not to be confused with people who just prefer being alone).

The **antisocial** personality is a con man (or woman). They can be charming and believable, but in reality, they are liars and want

101

to use you for what they can get out of you. They have no regard for ethics, rules, the rights of others, or even the law. They lack a conscience, are deceitful, and manipulate and exploit others for their own gain, and this includes sex and money. They may steal things or be involved in drugs, even dealing them.

Sometimes we encounter people who have these traits. They deny wrongdoing and rationalize their actions — like the guy who took his roommate's iPad and said, when confronted by the roommate, "I didn't steal it; I just borrowed it." Dealing with these people is very difficult, as they are slippery, evasive, and tough. You may know perfectly well that they did something wrong, but when you confront them, they are tricky and verbally skilled enough to turn the situation around, so that you end up feeling that you are the one at fault!

These people are often good-looking and intelligent enough to stay just this side of the law throughout life. They can be successful, but sometimes, down the road, their luck runs out, when they are arrested, their marriages derail due to infidelity, or they are terminated from their jobs for fraud, embezzlement, ethics charges, or a host of other offenses.

✗ Tool:

While *neurotics* cause themselves pain, *character-flawed* people inflict pain on everybody else. If you encounter a character-flawed person, the best option is to leave them alone, if possible. If you get involved with them, you may think you can change them, but chances are you will fail. They would have to acknowledge that they have a problem and want to change, and unfortunately, usually, they don't.

Difficult people behave in ways that make life difficult for the rest of us. This is because they have maladaptive ways of defending themselves against their feelings. If someone's behavior is consistently unreliable or if you are uncomfortable with their behavior toward you, think hard about whether this relationship is right for you.

Acting Out is a defense mechanism that involves behaving according to your basic desires or impulses without being aware of the emotions behind it. In Chapter 10, we will discuss acting out sexually, like Nora did, under the influence of alcohol. Because alcohol loosens our inhibitions, it can also cause us to act out hostile and aggressive feelings that we may not even realize we have. One young man, who was normally quiet and reserved, discovered this when he got drunk one night and acted out intense anger toward a friend by yelling, calling him names, and trying to engage him in a fight.

Some people act out whether or not they are under the influence of drugs or alcohol. They may suddenly change from being a reliable friend to one who is unreliable, saying things or acting in ways that we never saw before. They may get involved with activities or people with whom we do not feel comfortable. One young woman was devastated when her best friend "came on" to her boyfriend, acting out her unconscious feelings of competition, jealousy, and hostility. And those whose deeds resulted in the deaths of Tyler and Megan — the college student and the teen-age girl whose suicides after Internet victimization are mentioned in Chapter 2 —must bear the painful emotional burden of their acting out for the rest of their lives.

Passive Aggressive Behavior is a defense mechanism some people use as a way to deal with anger. Passive aggressives act out anger through indirect actions, such as "forgetting," procrastinating, saying negative things behind another's back, or being deliberately inefficient. When someone is acting this way toward you, you may know something is wrong, but you cannot be clear about why you are feeling angry. Passive aggressives skirt around issues, never saying anything directly, but their inaction is a way of expressing their anger toward you. They will avoid making a commitment to do something, but won't say plainly that they don't want to do it. It's a kind of game-playing, a way to gain control. Here are some typical interactions with passive aggressives:

Sid: "Do you want to go to the movie at 7?"

Barry: "I don't know; I have a lot of work. Let me get back to you."

When 6:45 PM came, Barry was nowhere to be seen and did not answer his cell phone. Barry did not really want to go but did not say this directly. Instead, he "said" it through his behavior of avoidance and unreliability. This left Sid feeling confused and angry.

Bree ended up in an angry confrontation with **Karen**, one of her roommates, who repeatedly "forgot" to pay her share into the common fund used by the roommates to buy the things they shared, like the printer ink cartridges. Karen also procrastinated doing clean-up duties when it was her turn, and when she finally did them, the result was decidedly half-baked. Karen's behavior was passive aggressive—forgetting, procrastinating, and doing chores poorly. Bree's reaction of anger was what most people feel in response to this. She had stored up so much resentment toward Karen for not contributing her fair share that her emotions, when vented, were out of control.

Janice and **Carol** belonged to the same group, but Janice held a grudge against Carol for dating Janice's old boyfriend. When Janice organized a birthday party for a friend at a local restaurant, she told Carol to be there at 9 PM. When Carol arrived, the group was no longer there; they had gone elsewhere to continue the celebration. Carol later learned that the party had started at 7 PM, and by 9 PM, the group was long gone. Janice was jealous, pure and simple, and her passive aggressive behavior was her way of getting even with Carol.

Steve, Rick and **Taylor** were assigned to work as a group for a class project. As the deadline drew closer, Rick had not done his part. When Steve confronted him, he said he was "working on it but had been involved in other things." Finally, the night before, the guys agreed to get together to finalize it. When Rick failed to show up, Steve called him. Rick said that other things had come up, and he still did not have his piece done. This infuriated Steve and Taylor, who had to scramble to finish the job in order to avoid being penalized for Rick's failure. Rick did not want to do the project and acted this out indirectly like Barry did by "disappearing" when needed. Steve and Taylor were careful never to work with Rick again, instead, choosing a reliable "team player."

Tool:

Passive aggressive people may be unaware of their anger that is coming out sideways toward someone else. If you feel that you have been "side-swiped" by someone, confront them — but only after you get a grip on your anger. If they deny responsibility but you still have to work with them, at least for the time being, try to make arrangements that will minimize the harm they can potentially do. You may have to accept that you'll have to pick up the slack if they haven't done their part. If you can make a change and get them off your team, do it.

EMOTIONAL SUFFERING

Of all of the human emotions, anxiety, shame, and humiliation are among the most painful and jealousy, envy, and anger the most toxic. People and situations can trigger these feelings, which we all have to learn to manage.

Anxiety

Anxiety is a kind of fear that is hard-wired into the human consciousness. In order to survive, early humans like other animals, used fear in an adaptive way. The mechanism was the "fight or flight response." Fear released chemicals that heightened awareness, sharpened focus, and increased physical strength and readiness to hunt prey, fight enemies, or run away. These reactions prepared them for danger and helped them to survive, whether by fighting or fleeing.

Most of us have experienced the physical sensations of fear/anxiety that our ancestors felt. Our heart rate and breathing speed up. We feel a churning sensation in the stomach. Our palms feel sweaty and our muscles tense. We feel physically keyed up, agitated, and jittery, like when we have had too much caffeine. Our thoughts race; we are highly alert and ready for action.

To a degree, anxiety *is* adaptive. Anxiety about a test or exam makes us study harder, so that we can do well. If we're anxious about a job, a college interview, or a first date, it helps us to take extra care in our appearance and manner. But too much anxiety can be harmful. It can be disproportionate to the situation and can bring us considerable distress, both physical and emotional. We eat too much or not at all. We cannot sleep. Funny physical symptoms, aches, and pains, can worry us. We lose peace of mind. Anxiety overtakes our sense of well-being and interferes with our daily lives. We find ourselves feeling an overwhelming sense of doom and pessimism. Everything feels negative. Everything in our lives seems catastrophic. Even worse, this unmanageable anxiety can bring about the very outcome we feared— a self-fulfilling prophecy! Let's look at different types of anxiety.

One type of anxiety is called *situational anxiety*. Life is full of anxiety-provoking situations. Examples are exams, theatrical performances or athletic competitions. Most of the time, when we feel anxious about a situation, we can identify the object that we fear—the test, interview, first date, term project, or competition. Knowing what we are concerned about, we can prepare accordingly. Usually, we can handle this type of anxiety.

Sometimes, however, our anxiety level about a situation goes off the chart and we are agitated beyond what we feel is a normal level. This anxiety is different than the usual kind we are able to handle. We may recognize that there is something different about this situation.

The difference is that beyond the actual circumstances we face, the situation has a strong *perceptual* component. That means we are thinking that the situation is more threatening than it may be in reality. This is because the situation has tapped into something that has a deeper emotional meaning for us. It is this perceptual part that is adding unrealistic intensity. Like the child who fears there is a monster in the dark, we exaggerate the perceived threat. Even though the parent knows that the child's fear is unrealistic, it usually does little good to tell him that there is no monster there. However, giving the child a "blankie" to protect him can do wonders. The blanket becomes endowed with magical powers to protect the child from the monster. This comforts him enough to help him manage his fear. So where is the "blankie" for us big kids? What can give us the emotional power to shrink our internal monsters and fears to a realistic size?

✗ Tools:

1. Try to identify both the *real* and *perceptual* components of whatever is making you feel anxious. You cannot control the *reality*, but you can work on the perceptual piece by figuring out its meaning. What hidden vulnerabilities are being stirred in you? Ask yourself: What could be the worst outcome of this situation, and what would be the consequences if it occurs? Would your life be really derailed, or realistically, would you be able to handle it? Make a plan of action for this feared outcome in order to reassure yourself, regain a sense of control, and reduce your general sense of apprehension.

2. Someone observed that 95 percent of the things we worry about never happen. Take life one day at a time, and avoid worrying about situations that may never come about.

3. Here is a specific formula that may help you—an adaptation that comes from the Navy Seals, who train to overcome their fear of drowning using these basic techniques that really work:

A. Set little goals.

B. Imagine success and rehearse it in your mind.

C. Use positive Self-Talk.

D. Focus on breathing to relax.

4. Are you the philosophical type? Here is wisdom from an anonymous source, who really got to the essence of anxiety:

Fear knocked.
Courage answered.
There was nothing there.

In addition to *situational anxiety*, there are other kinds of anxiety, like *social anxiety*, which makes someone generally fearful of being around people. Those with this condition have difficulty making friends. Instead of pleasurable companionship, being with other people gives them a sense of uneasiness and self-doubt.

Then there can be a more diffuse or *general* type of anxiety that makes people feel anxious most of the time about a variety of life issues, such as relationships, finances, career, or just the future. Fear dominates their lives so completely that they end up worrying about everything.

It can be hard to understand what is behind anxiety. Many anxious people are perfectionists, driven to please or succeed. Their perfectionism can lead to compulsive behavior as a way to control the anxiety, but this is rarely completely successful. Others have an intense fear of failure, rejection, or abandonment by others, such as parents, teachers, coaches, friends, bosses, or a significant other on whom they depend for support.

For people with significant anxiety, fear can impede their taking even reasonable risks to try out new things, reach out to others, or grow to be more independent. Life becomes narrow. They stick to the tried and true and miss out on potentially enriching new experiences. In some cases, anxiety is so severe that depression results.

When we find that that we are keyed up all the time and anxiety has become unmanageable, what can we do? Here are some strategies for both anxiety and depression, which often go together:

✷ Tools:

1. First, make sure there is no physical reason for your anxiety. Reduce or eliminate caffeine, which is in soda as well as coffee and tea. Increase intake of foods containing L-tryptophan, a substance that is a precursor to the brain chemical, serotonin. Serotonin promotes sleep and relaxation and elevates our mood. Turkey breast and dairy products, such as yogurt and cheese, are good sources of this. If you still feel the physical signs of anxiety and cannot find a reason why, have a medical checkup. Certain conditions, such as thyroid disorders, may be masquerading as anxiety.

2. Get regular exercise. If you are really anxious, get in an extra workout. Exercise has been proven medically to reduce anxiety, improve sleep, and elevate mood.

3. Try a technique called "thought stopping." When the anxiety-provoking thought comes into your mind, stop the thought and replace it with one that

doesn't make you anxious. While you are doing this, focus on your breathing and meditate on something calming, like a nature scene. Begin at the top of your head and progressively relax every part of your body.

4. Develop a self-soothing technique. This is a skill that takes practice. Discover a method that helps you calm down when you are keyed up. Do a progressive relaxation technique while imagining yourself in a safe and pleasant place, or take action to change your environment.

5. Get involved in a constructive activity that takes you out of yourself. To get the most "bang from your buck," volunteer to help those in need—lonely senior citizens, the homeless, or women who are escaping domestic violence, to name a few. Their lives and troubles will give you perspective on your own. Chapter 6 talks more about the healing power of helping others.

6. Try distraction! Go on a walk, talk to a friend, watch a movie, or listen to music that is relaxing

or upbeat. Remember getting candy from the pediatrician after you got a shot? The candy distracted you, and you stopped crying. Distraction works for everyone, not just toddlers! It can disrupt a cycle of anxiety by getting us involved with something else. How about a relaxing bath! Sound crazy? Winston Churchill often took them when he was Prime Minister of England during World War II.

7. There are some good self-help tools.

A. Check out E-couch, an online self-help tool for anxiety disorders as well as depression:

http://ecouch.anu.edu.au/welcome

B. Clinicians have some tools to help them quickly assess symptoms in patients. One is the Generalized Anxiety Disorder checklist:

http://www.phqscreeners.com/pdfs/03_GAD-7/English.pdf

If you check the higher numbers on most of the questions and you are not getting very far using the tools in this book, it may be time to get together with a professional.

C. The books of the late Dr. Claire Weekes continue to help millions. Here are two of them: *Hope and Help for Your Nerves* and *Peace from Nervous Suffering*.

8. Find a hobby. Churchill took up painting after age 40 and found that it provided great psychological relief from anxiety and depression. He read, wrote, and even managed to work on his painting a little during World War II. These creative activities soothed and distracted him, helping him to remain calm and focused as he inspired his people and led them through the horrors of the War. At an appropriate time in life, you might enjoy the companionship of a pet—a great antidote to loneliness and anxiety.

9. If the anxiety still feels unmanageable, or if you are also getting depressed, there are resources available to help. Talking to a counselor, spiritual advisor, or doctor like a psychiatrist can help you get to the bottom of the problem. Counseling offers very effective strategies to cope with anxiety, and both anxiety and depression can often be helped by a small amount of a non-addicting medication, like an antidepressant. For severe anxiety and/or depression, counseling and medication together make a winning combination, taking the edge off of symptoms and getting you back on track. Do not be afraid or ashamed of getting medical help. This does not mean that you are crazy, weird or defective. The mind is a part of the body. If you had a broken arm, you would have it treated. Treating emotional symptoms and maintaining our mental health is no less important.

Shame and Humiliation

When she was a graduate student, **Ann** was the head teaching fellow for her department in a university that prided itself on open inquiry without prejudice. The teaching fellows under her supervision were responsible for grading student papers produced in a large undergraduate survey course. When a freshman wrote a paper that departed from standard theories, his teaching fellow gave the paper an F and wrote "Barf" on it and nothing else. The student, devastated with shame by the grade and remark, asked to meet with Ann. When Ann read the paper, she found it a thoughtful treatise, even though it espoused theories that were out of favor at the time. Other than that, she found no basis for giving the paper a failing grade. She and the professor who taught the course both concluded that the teaching fellow's reaction was out of line, and the professor reversed the grade. In a meeting with the teaching fellow, they pointed out that he had shown bias and a lapse in judgment. The teaching fellow was highly offended and said so. He was at the top of his class in medical school and could not believe anyone would question his judgment. A discussion followed with the student in hopes of repairing the damage that had been done.

This teaching fellow had intensely overreacted to the student's unorthodox point of view. Maybe it was to assert power or to prove he was superior to the student, or maybe he was projecting all of his own fears of inadequacy onto the student. Whatever it was, when his bias was pointed out, he reacted defensively with narcissistic rage—a type of rage we feel when we have sustained a direct blow to our ego, self-esteem, or pride – and chose to quit rather than reflect on the possible truths in the criticism. He had been used to being regarded as one of the "brightest and the best." Such confrontation was a major wound, and his self-esteem was bleeding from humiliation and shame. Rage was his emotional bandage, if an immature and ineffective one. Quitting gave him an escape from a painful situation, but he learned little in the process.

Shame is such a painful feeling that most people work hard to hide it. Whether it is difficult family circumstances, troubling life experiences, or poor college preparation, we fear that our deficiencies are glaringly apparent to everyone we meet. We feel ashamed of ourselves and want to hide our perceived inadequacies or redouble our efforts to overcome them. Remember Alexis' boss in Chapter 5? His strong denial probably covered a sense of shame.

The student in the above story felt intense shame about his paper, but an intervention by a wise head teaching fellow and professor softened the blow. A failing grade is only one possible cause of shame. Anything that emotionally leaves us feeling different, separate from, and inferior to others can trigger this feeling. When others call attention to our differences, we can feel humiliated—attacked in a place where we are vulnerable. Whether it is our height, weight, clothes, intellectual achievements, money or the lack of it, ethnicity, family situation, religion, medical disability, unusual life experiences, the neighborhood we come from, or the label we held since childhood when others called us "nerd," "jock," or worse — whatever makes us feel self-conscious and "out of it" can evoke feelings of shame.

Marguerite lived with her affluent grandparents and attended a prestigious day school on the West Coast. Her mother had Alzheimer's and lived in poverty, getting limited nursing help through an indigents' service agency. Every weekend, Marguerite drove to the other side of town to spend time with her mother, who was unable to recognize her. Often her mother lost control of her bladder and bowel, and Marguerite had to clean this up. She was so ashamed of her mother that she never told her friends about her, and, of course, never took any of her friends over to meet her. When they asked, she just said that her mother was "not well."

Does there have to be shame in being different? Look at people who seem to have dealt successfully with this. Instead of feeling ashamed of being different and trying hard to be like the group, they find some useful way of dealing with whatever makes them different. Here is such a success story.

Rita had a big nose and came from the "wrong side of the tracks." When she entered a small prestigious school, there were only two other students that did not come from Kings Bluff, the prestigious area of town. Rather than letting these differences erode her confidence, she emphasized her beautiful hair, long eyelashes, and considerable talent in voice and piano. She became accepted by the "in" group and was invited to join the most prestigious sorority. Somehow her big nose and where she lived never seemed to be a problem to her privileged friends. By contrast, for **Janice**, another student from Rita's less privileged neighborhood, the fact that she did not live in King's Bluff became an insurmountable psychological issue, leaving her feeling ashamed and left out. Janice's shame pervaded her social life. The issue of social status became the center of her emotions, while Rita skipped lightly over it and did not let it get in her way.

Wrestling with our differences can be a challenge. It is difficult to examine, much less, accept them without shame, especially if others reject or disparage us for these differences. How can we manage *shame*?

✗ Tools:

1. We cannot control how others react to us, but, as the author, Deepak Chopra, wisely pointed out, we have a choice in how we react to others — and

whether we react to them at all. We also have a choice in how we react to ourselves and our own differences. So if you are struggling with differences, try this little experiment. Look at yourself in a full-length mirror, getting a view of the complete you. There's much more to you than just the thing that is different, however ashamed it makes you feel. Look at your good qualities and don't minimize them. Everyone has strengths and weaknesses. Don't let shame about a difference overshadow everything that is great about you. Write down those positives. Rita could have focused on her big nose instead of her musical talents. Instead, she used these talents, making others focus on them too. The nose was just one element of Rita, a small part of the entire package, an aspect of her individuality. It may take you time and patience to accept your differences and learn to put them in their proper proportion. But acceptance of them is part of your Individuation process—something distinctive that can become a source of strength and wisdom for your life.

2. If you have a physical attribute about which you feel ashamed, humor, the highest and most adaptive defense mechanism, can diminish it and please others. The great comedian Jimmy Durante referred to his trademark giant nose as the "Big Schnozzolla." He once joked, "My nose isn't big; I just happen to have a very small head!"

A television news reporter interviewed a Vietnam veteran who had such severe facial scars from an explosion that his features were virtually lost. Rather than withdraw, give up, or lash out when others recoiled, he used his changed appearance to inspire others. When he visited burn wards in hospitals, patients knew he understood what they were going through. His upbeat attitude gave them courage and hope. When he spoke to children, they often asked him what had happened to his face. He replied that he had used his mouth to get a French fry out of a pot of boiling oil and did not recommend this method. Everyone laughed when a child asked, "Did you get one?"

3. Whether through humor or another approach, work to detach yourself from the shame and put it into an emotional "box" outside of you where you can examine it when your emotions are not in turmoil. You can greatly decrease or even eliminate this feeling!

4. Cultivate an internal "wise leader" who is a part of you. Did you have a family member or an adult friend you looked up to as a child? Model your internal "wise leader" after that person, and use it to help you, just as if you had called in a consultant to advise you on how to fix your computer.

5. Think about where the shame is coming from. If memories come to you, write them down in a journal. If the shame comes from childhood experiences and background, look at the past through "new eyes"—i.e., those of your "wise leader." Now as an adult rather than a child, approach the wounded, frightened, and ashamed child inside of you. Befriend it and guide it to a safer, better place—the place where you have arrived today through hard

work and commitment to overcoming the obstacles of your early life. Realize that although we can't change the past, we can change our view of it. This may take time, but we can gradually "re-work" it emotionally, as we build our lives through education, friendships, spiritual growth, and work. No longer held hostage by shame or the feeling that we need somehow to apologize for ourselves and the past, we have integrated the past into the fabric of our lives and understand that it has given us a depth and perspective that we can use to empathize with others.

Shame and the Issue of "Class"

Sometimes people have uncomfortable feelings, even embarrassment or shame, about the circumstances in which they were raised. This was part of what bothered Janice in the above story. Differences in social class are a *relative* thing. In an old-style monarchy, the king feels subordinate only to God. An earl feels subordinate to the king, a baronet to the earl, and so forth down the hierarchy. In modern society a middle-class person may feel that he ranks below a rich and influential one. A non-college educated person may feel he has less status than someone with a college degree. An apprentice feels subordinate to a master craftsman, a medical resident to an attending physician, and a freshman to a senior.

We all bring our backgrounds and our feelings about it into any new social situation. How we handle new social situations depends on many factors, including emotional resilience, general confidence level, and personality style. In this era, social distinctions are more flexible than ever and can be bridged in many ways. More than 70 years ago Edward VIII abdicated his right to the throne of England in order to marry a commoner, Wallis Simpson, and Prince William, a future king, married Kate Middleton, a young woman of middle class means. These stories remind us that personal qualities, education, and achievement can help supersede social barriers.

In our society, we may react with jealousy and envy, or we may idealize those of "higher" social standing because of the power that can accompany money or privilege. Either reaction involves attributing to them superhuman traits, which, in fact, they may not possess. If circumstances bring us into possible contact with wealthy or prominent people, we may try to avoid them because we feel awkward or inferior. But this is just another type of *projection*. Those people are just human beings, who, like us, have positive and negative attributes, and who are just *looking for support*.

Different responses to feelings about family origins and social status emerge from the stories of two young women who came to college from very different backgrounds, **Linda** and **Consuela**.

Linda came from a broken home and a family with limited means. She and her sister were raised by a mother who cleaned houses. When she came to college, she had few clothes and no other possessions that could liven up her dormitory room. Nonetheless, she had a magnanimous personality, a cheerful "can-do" attitude, and sense of humor that gave her a perspective on her background. She told friends the story of the time her mother drove their "junker" car to a service station and asked the attendant, "Can you give me a windshield wiper for my car?" He replied, "Sounds like an even trade to me." Her friends howled. No one ever made fun of her appearance or circumstances. Instead of feeling ashamed or embarrassed about her background, somehow, she had been able to integrate it and not let it give her an excuse to avoid friendship.

By contrast, **Consuela**, another student, was an aristocratic Venezuelan woman, whose father was in the oil business. She did not interact comfortably with others in her dorm, quickly moving through the dining hall to her room. Outside of her classes, she associated with few women and dated only certain men of means. Most of classmates did not like her, but one, **Ginny**, decided to try to get to know her. It was not easy going at first.

Consuela's affectations built a strong defensive wall around her—one that was not easy to overcome. As Ginny got to know her, she learned that Consuela was, in fact, a rather lonely, insecure, and self-conscious person whose life had been insulated by wealth. Her parents had warned her that people would only be interested in her because of her money, but she found that this aspect of her life made most people avoid her because of their discomfort. She was, in fact, reluctant to have anyone get to know her well, because they might see flaws and reject her. Underneath her façade of confidence and superiority, she struggled with doubts about whether she had anything to offer other than her status.

Consuela's case shows that money, beauty, privilege, and other external factors that seem to be significant advantages in life can also mask feelings of inadequacy and imperfection and be an obstacle to friendship.

Tool:

If you are in a new group, such as a college class, there may be a person who seems intimidating — a movie star, a member of a famous political or royal family, or perhaps just someone who is very well-to-do. Rather than shying away, consider stepping out of your comfort zone to get to know such people a little. Initiate a conversation to "test the waters." By their response, you will know quickly whether or not they are open to new relationships. Perhaps they are reluctant, because they fear that others are only judging them by these externals. Maybe they are caught up in the Money Shadow, which makes money or social status the yardstick for measuring others, but maybe they are not. You might be surprised to find out how isolated and lonely they feel because others are uncomfortable with their celebrity status. They may feel that their social position and wealth are obstacles, rather than advantages, to developing meaningful relationships with others. When you try to open up communication, you might find a new friendship that is based on shared values and interests, qualities that are deeper than social status or wealth position.

Jealousy and Envy—the Green-Eyed Monster

Jealousy and envy are among the most virulent of human emotions, invading our souls and relationships like a deadly virus.

These emotions often involve the psychological defense mechanisms of *denial* and *projection*, which we saw before with Dawn. But sometimes the jealousy and envy involve things other than romantic relationships, as seen in this story.

Kim, an Asian American, was ecstatic when she was admitted to a prestigious university. Although she and her family tried to restrict this news to close relatives and a few special friends, word got out. Suddenly, Kim found that her two best friends at school were avoiding her. Even when she initiated conversations, they were cold and curt in their replies. She asked them what was wrong, but all they said was "Nothing." Kim talked about this with another friend, who confirmed that the girls were jealous, even though Kim had been careful not to change her behavior or flaunt her success. Over time, regrettably, little changed, and in spite of Kim's best efforts, the old friendship with the two girls gradually ended, leaving Kim disappointed and confused but grateful for the consistency of the third friend.

How can the behavior of the friends be best understood? Beneath their jealous and envy, there may have been unspoken hurts and pain. Perhaps Kim's college admission had triggered their competitive feelings. In comparing themselves to her, the friends may have felt diminished by her success. Perhaps cultural influences or the same type of competitive feelings had led their families to say something negative or critical to the girls, such as, "Why couldn't you have studied harder and gotten into ____ college like

130

Kim did?" Perhaps the friends or families had idealized the university to which Kim had been admitted and unfairly feared that Kim had changed or would change because of her admission there, despite her constancy as a friend. The truth is that Kim *was* changed and will likely continue to be changed by her admission to the college. Any significant occurrence changes us in some way and transforms us into a new person, we hope for the better. In Kim's case, despite her friends' fears, her good fortune did not necessarily mean that she was doomed to metamorphose into a monster—a totally different person, detached from her family, friends, and community, devoid of her old values, becoming suddenly a snob with no time for old friends. Unfortunately, her friends did not give her a chance to demonstrate this. They remained stuck in their jealousy and missed out on an opportunity to grow.

It can be very hard not to feel jealous when someone else gets a prize that we wanted. How can we not feel angry when our romantic interest chooses someone else over us, or when we feel that our favorite teacher prefers another student's work to ours. We think we deserved the recognition that was given to someone else. There can be a sibling rivalry aspect to the emotional triangle that is in play between you, the person who beat you out in some way, and the reward you didn't get. It can also be complicated when the situation is reversed – you have some success or gain that makes someone else resent you. What can you do when others feel jealous or envious of you? What can you do when you feel this way toward them?

✗ Tools:

1. When others behave this way toward you, realize that they, not you, are responsible for their feelings and emotional reactions. Do not feel guilty about your success, and do not feel that you have to make up for whatever you achieved that they did not. Instead, if the relationship is important to you, try, as Kim did, not to react in anger ("How dare they be such jerks!"). If you can, try to remain consistent in your behavior and habits with them. In time, their fears or resentment may diminish as they grow to accept the new you. If they do not, at least you have tried.

2. When you catch yourself feeling this way toward others, see if you are projecting some idealized part of yourself onto the person and comparing yourself negatively in the process. If you can consciously recognize the projection, you may begin to see it fall away.

3. There is wisdom in this ancient Chinese saying:

He who gets what he wants is successful.
He who wants what he gets is happy.

The fact is: there will always be someone who is smarter, better looking, richer, more accomplished, luckier, etc. than we are. Turn your attention to your own good qualities and work on developing and improving them. Cultivate an attitude of thankfulness for what has been given to you. Work on your deficits but do not dwell on the past or situations you cannot change.

4. Feeling envious of someone who seems to get all the breaks? You may assume that such people are floating through life without any problems, but do you really know the intricacies of their lives? Are you projecting this notion of an idealized life onto them? The reality is that no one gets through life unscathed. Everyone is tested, some more than others.

5. *You never know your luck!* One door may be closed to you, but other doors will open. You cannot know how your life would have been different if only you had gotten what you desired. It may be that the outcome you desired would have been harmful for you in the end, bringing you unhappiness or stress instead of greater comfort and happiness. Similarly the outcome you thought you didn't want may lead to relationships and circumstances that enrich your life. Just as in the college selection process, in which students grow to love the college that loves them, be receptive to the open doors in your life.

6. Try to develop a gracious attitude toward the other person's good fortune. Using humor can defuse anxieties on both sides.

7. If jealousy or envy becomes a major emotional obstacle, consider talking to a counselor. Counseling can help you understand and resolve the issues evoking these feelings, so that they no longer interfere with your relationships and leave you feeling unhappy.

Anger and Rage

To be alive is to feel anger. Sometimes our anger feels justified, but sometimes it can be irrational or excessive. Once in a while, we can really lose it and become enraged. Learn to recognize what anger feels like physically. When we understand those physical signs, we can begin to learn how to defuse anger, so that it does not cause mental stress and physical problems. Connecting the physical signs with our emotional state alerts us to a problem that we need to address before the feelings escalate into rage and we do something that we later regret. If *anger* is a small lawn fire, *rage* is scorched earth.

Jack lit into his roommate, **Brian**, in an attack that seemed to come out of nowhere. He had a litany of complaints, most of which seemed trivial—leaving a towel on the floor or changing the location of a party. Brian listened, stunned. Who was this alien that had taken over his roommate? **Ted** witnessed this confrontation and told Jack to take a walk with him. "What's going on with you? You were way out of line and you really need to apologize," he told Jack. As they talked, Jack began to realize that he had been holding in a lot of anger toward Brian over a number of weeks. A lot of little things had been piling up. He had just gone along on issues when he felt he should have said no. He felt Brian was too controlling about how things were shared within the rooming group. The kicker was that everybody else took a turn, albeit grudgingly, to clean the bathroom, everyone that is, except Brian. He seemed to get whatever he wanted without too much regard for others. Plus, there was a girl that Brian had "scooped" from Jack. That had been the last straw. When Ted asked why he had never said anything, Jack realized that he needed to take responsibility for his feelings and not just do nothing when he felt Brian was out of bounds. This incident, in fact, helped all of the roommates realize how much anger they too had stored up about Brian's behavior. They held a roommate meeting to address the bathroom and other problems. The meeting was hard to do, but the group negotiated some compromises everyone could accept and remained friends. As far as the girl was concerned, Brian had no idea that Jack had been interested, and neither did the girl. Jack learned fast to take a risk and let the next girl know he was interested.

Usually, someone has done something to trigger our anger. Maybe, like Jack, we are envious or jealous or ready to explode after a long "slow burn." In other cases, our anger is a response when someone else's behavior has felt hostile. As we have seen from some of the examples above, there are hundreds of ways in which other people's actions or failure to act leaves us feeling angry. Their viewpoints or the way they convey them feels offensive. Maybe they have acted aggressively toward us through sarcastic, caustic, or humiliating put-downs. They may have made jokes at our expense or made an untoward comment about someone or something we value. Sometimes their offensive behavior is more indirectly hostile, or passive aggressive.

They "forgot" an appointment, delayed getting back to us on something until it was too late, or tried to subvert us behind our back. We recognize from the churning in our gut that we are boiling mad, and we are ready for revenge. Before we explode like Jack, ready to embark on a scorched earth campaign, what can we do?

✗ Tools:

1. Get control of your emotions. Revisit the **Emotions Scale (p. 88).** Work out or take a walk. Distract yourself or use your self-soothing techniques to calm down. Let some time go by. Talk to a friend.

2. Once you feel in control, ask yourself if the intensity of your anger is valid, or if it might be out of proportion to the situation. If it feels out of proportion, are there other feelings beneath it — humiliation, disappointment, rejection, or something else?

3. Consider the person who has offended you. Is the relationship a close one in which you can discuss your feelings (using the "I" statements) at a later time? If so, find a time (sooner rather than later) to

discuss the problem, listen to the other person's side, and try to come to a satisfactory resolution. If the relationship is distant, read on.

4. Some people have the gift of wit and humor. Do you? This can be an effective way to deal with a "put down" while defusing your own anger. The best humor is at our own expense. A Southerner from a small town in Alabama responded this way to a Northern friend who referred to Southerners as "dumb rednecks": "Yep, down there, we're so dumb we think that Taco Bell is a Mexican phone company."

5. Is it unfeasible to deal with the other person directly? Write an imaginary letter to him or her expressing all of your feelings; then destroy it. You might be surprised at the relief you feel.

6. Is it hard to manage your emotions? Consider getting a "consult" from counselor or doctor. Give them some examples in which you were out of control. They can help you figure out what is pushing your buttons.

7. Do you prefer to get group support? Check out Emotions Anonymous, a 12 Step Program patterned after Alcoholics Anonymous:

www.emotionsanonymous.org

Their website states, "Our fellowship is composed of people who come together in weekly meetings for the purpose of working toward recovery from emotional difficulties."

Loss

Loss is an archetypal human experience. Everyone loses someone or something important at some time in life. People we love die. We may lose our possessions, money, or health. The longer we live, the more losses we sustain. As Indian philosophy teaches, nothing in life is certain. In fact, everything in life is uncertain except suffering. No doubt about it.

The feeling of loss is tangible and visceral as well as emotional. We feel an emptiness that was not there before. We may feel a gut-level ache when we lose something of value. Have you ever lost your wallet? You probably felt that sinking feeling. We may feel literally sick when we don't get a reward or outcome that we have worked hard to achieve. Much worse, we seem to feel our heart physically breaking when a family or love relationship derails. All of these losses create a hole in our lives. Our response to loss is grief.

Some losses, though inconvenient, can be fairly easily recovered. We can replace our wallets, credit cards, and driver's license. If we make a mistake managing our money, we can learn from that and adjust. Most of the time, we can get medical care and be cured of our ailments. If we move to a new place, we can make new friends who can help replace the lost companionship.

Other losses are permanent and more difficult to accept. Death is final. The breakdown of a relationship may also feel irreversible. Our failure to achieve a goal brings the death of a dream or fantasy. To heal from these, we need to develop a broader perspective on life that will help us understand and integrate loss into the overall fabric of our lives.

Buddhist philosophy has much to say on how we can end our suffering and achieve peace. It teaches that suffering comes from desire, and peace comes from giving up our desires. According to Buddhism, it is our attachments that ensnare us in a never-ending cycle of disappointment, loss, and suffering.

This philosophy has wisdom. But it is only half the story, for it is also true that our attachments — to our faith, life's work, art or music, families, and friends — can enrich our lives, help us grow, and be a source of joy, comfort, and meaning. But we also must accept that outside of our faith, life may give us things that it can later take away. The challenge is to enjoy the things we are given without developing an all-consuming attachment to them. In the end, we all die, relinquishing all of our possessions and relationships. If we can practice giving up control, it can help us accept the totality of life. To live is to die. To gain is to lose. Everything is constantly changing, but, according to Buddhism, nothing is lost in the universe, including those we love. Death converts living things from one form of being to another. Our earthly remains become dust, but our souls endure within those who love us and beyond. The same is true for our strivings in life. Whether or not these remain after we are gone, the challenge is to enjoy relationships and the process of building something or working to achieve something meaningful while maintaining a degree of distance from the outcome.

Whatever form our loss takes, over time, we may find that something has occurred that diminishes the pain surrounding it. We have gone through various emotional stages to acceptance. The story about the loss becomes a narrative with meaning, and there may be even more. Within the death, there is life. Like the new growth on a branch that has been pruned, the loss has made room in our lives for something new to grow.

✳ Tool:

If your grief becomes prolonged, and you feel engulfed with sadness, this may be clinical depression, a medical condition for which you may need help. Try the techniques in this book to manage it, but if you cannot, call upon professionals to help.

Depression

Depression is a common problem in young people. It's not to be confused with the "down in the dumps" we all get from time to time. Those feelings usually pass in a day or two, but sometimes they don't. Something changes, and you can find yourself spinning into a cloud of darkness, which is clinical depression.

Depression is a painful emotional state that can cloud our thinking and pervade everything we do. We have no balance or perspective. Everything seems negative and hopeless, and we can feel helpless about our lives. Winston Churchill endured depression most of his life. He called it his "black dog." In those days before skilled counseling and antidepressant medication, he took walks for exercise or engaged in hobbies, like building his brick wall, sketching, or painting, in order to manage these episodes. Those strategies can be helpful but sometimes they are simply not enough. Think of a Depression Scale from 1 to 10, with 1 being mild to 10 being an emergency. The *Tools* section will offer strategies for dealing with all levels of depression.

⚒ Tools:

1. If you are feeling depressed, here is a brief online depression assessment tool. It is no substitute for a clinical evaluation by a qualified professional, but if you take it honestly, and answer "yes" to five or more questions, you may be suffering from clinical depression and need professional help:

   http://depression.about.com/cs/diagnosis/l/bldepscreenquiz.htm

2. The National Institute of Mental Health's website has a wealth of information on depression, including a more expanded list of symptoms and resources for help:

   http://www.nimh.nih.gov/health/publications/depression/complete-index.shtml#pub3

3. If you become overwhelmed with feelings of anxiety, panic, blues that never seem to get better, sleep or concentration problems, fatigue, indifference, or even hopelessness and helplessness, these feelings are signaling trouble. A feature of depression is that it keeps people from seeking help, because it makes them unable to believe that anything will help them. The truth is that depression is treatable and effective help is available. So even if it's hard to feel it will be of any use, make yourself fight that feeling and force yourself to look for help. If you are in college, call the college's Help Line, go to the counseling service, or, if you prefer, go to a community health professional. If you feel more comfortable with clerical counseling, seek that through the college or other sources.

4. If you recognize any of these symptoms or behaviors in someone you know, express your concern and talk about the points in Tool #1. They may need professional help. You can be the friend that helps them get it.

A Word about Suicide

Although everyone has thoughts about suicide, severe depression can distort our thinking and make us feel that there is no way out of our situation except to end our lives. If you are worried that someone may be feeling this way because of his comments or behavior, ask him calmly but *directly* **if he is feeling so down that he is thinking of harming himself.** You will not "push him over the edge." In fact, it is usually the opposite; people who attempt often say that they did so because no one cared enough to ask. Mayo Clinic's website has more information, including a list of questions you can ask **(http://www.mayoclinic.com/health/suicide/MH00058)**. If the person says "yes," or if *you* feel a strong urge to harm yourself, *it is time to get help now*.

✗ *Tools:*

1. Do not be alone. If you are with a suicidal person, do not leave him or her alone.

2. Call for help from an adult, like a parent, friend, or faculty advisor, or call the health services, a doctor, or 911, or get a friend to help you do these things.

3. Call the National Suicide Prevention Lifeline and talk to one of their trained counselors:
1-800-273-TALK (1-800-273-8255);
TTY: 1-800-799-4TTY (4889)

4. Go to the nearest hospital emergency room or clinic.

6. Suicide is a _permanent_ solution to a _temporary_ problem. Get a professional involved right away. They can help get you or your friend back on your feet.

- *Chapter Six* -

SUPER STRATEGIES for STORMY TIMES

Life gives us joy and pain, but during the Transition years, emotions in both directions seem to be heightened. Enjoy the good times and don't be overwhelmed by the down times. *They will pass, and life will right itself if you wait and use your Tools to work things out*! Try these strategies to help get back on track.

HELPING OTHERS

One of the most powerful self-help strategies for all kinds of emotional pain is to *help others*. Research has shown that reaching out to those in need can offer as much relief as counseling and/or medications, while boosting energy and immune systems, relieving stress, promoting relaxation, and increasing longevity! Practice helping others and make it part of your core values.

✷ Tool:

All colleges and communities offer ways you can help. Are you good with kids? Be a Big Brother or Sister or visit hospitalized children with cancer. Are you good in an area of study? Tutor those who aren't. Volunteer an hour to help the poor, elderly, sick, orphaned, disabled, the lonely and "forgotten." The need for your help is enormous. General hospitals, pediatric hospitals, nursing homes, hospice, veterans associations, libraries, schools, community centers, women's shelters, homeless shelters, soup kitchens, Habitat for Humanity, disaster relief agencies, animal shelters, churches and temples, food shelves, the military serving overseas and their families back home—the list is endless. William Penn said, "I expect to pass through life but once. If, therefore, there be any kindness I can show, or any good thing I can do for any fellow being, let me do it now... as I shall not pass this way again." Your gift of compassion will come back to you spiritually many times over.

HUMOR

Medical research has found that humor is a great healer, both of the mind and of the body. We do not understand why this is so, but its healing effects are complex and far-ranging, even extending the lives of patients with serious or terminal illnesses. Humor is contagious, especially when the humor makes light of our own weaknesses and flaws. As we have seen elsewhere, humor is a great way of dealing with our own inadequacies in a mature way that bonds us to others.

One person who used humor to counteract a difficult environment was the celebrated columnist, Art Buchwald. As a child growing up in poverty, Buchwald was harassed by a neighborhood bully, but responded by making jokes. The bully enjoyed the jokes so much that he ended up protecting Buchwald.

One of the most cherished comedians of all time was Bob Hope, who regaled his audiences with jokes about himself. Once, his frequent co-star, Bing Crosby, chided Hope about his expanding waist line. Hope replied, "The older you get, the tougher it is to lose weight, because by then your body and your fat are really good friends." A lover of golf, Hope had many things to say about this game. "I set out to play golf with the intention of shooting my age, but I shot my weight instead."

Look for the lightness in a situation as a way to cope with it. If you can poke fun at yourself, all the better, but avoid making fun of others. Did you stick your foot in your mouth? Talk about how tasty it is. Usually our gaffes seem more serious to us than they do to others. Remember that most people are more interested in their own lives and problems than they are in ours. By the way, sarcasm is best reserved for ideas; avoid using it against others. It will only alienate them and make you look (and feel) mean-spirited.

✷ Tool:

Down in the dumps? Check out a comedy movie or get a book of jokes. The Internet is an endless source of humor. Don't forget about puns, which, like other types of jokes, can be a welcome distraction and give an emotional lift. If you find some good ones, send them to friends.

Here are two winners from the International Pun Contest:

A group of chess enthusiasts checked into a hotel and were standing in the lobby discussing their recent tournament victories. After about an hour, the manager came out of the office and asked them to disperse. "But why?" they asked, as they moved off. "Because," he said, "I can't stand chess-nuts boasting in an open foyer."

A group of friars were behind on their belfry payments, so they opened up a small florist shop to raise funds. Since everyone liked to buy flowers from the men of God, a rival florist across town thought the competition was unfair. He asked the good fathers to close down, but they would not. He went back and begged the friars to close. They ignored him. So, the rival florist hired Hugh MacTaggart, the roughest and most vicious thug in town, to persuade the friars to close. Hugh beat up the friars and trashed their store, saying he'd be back if they didn't close up shop. Terrified, they did so, thereby proving that only Hugh can prevent florist friars.

FORGIVENESS

Sometimes people deal us particularly hard blows, often unde-served. We may not be able to remedy the situation, no matter how hard we try, and we are left devastated. First we may be stunned, and later, angry. Thinking about forgiveness is impos-sible; the injury is too fresh.

Forgiving a person who has hurt us can take a long time. Lingering anger can become a bitter root that gets established within our souls and invades our whole being. What Christianity teaches about forgiveness is a universal truth. Work to replace anger with understanding, compassion, and acceptance, if not love. Like this story illustrates, you will find that forgiveness can be life-changing.

Jo entered college from a difficult background. Her parents were ill-suited to one another and argued constantly. Her authoritarian father disciplined the children with a strap, while her mother remained cold and silent. The parents held a tight rein on the children, who could do nothing on weeknights and had a 10:00 PM curfew on Saturday night. The six siblings were constantly at war with each other, and when they graduated from high school, they scattered to the four corners of the world. Jo could not wait to get out of the family environment. From early life, she devel-oped a strategy of "escape." A disciplined student, she worked hard in high school, excelling in academic and extracurricular activities, and was accepted to a top-flight college thousands of miles from her home town. Even across the country was barely far enough away to suit her, and she resolved never to go home again. She was particularly angry toward her violent father with whom she severed communication completely. Opening the door to college, she closed the door on her unhappy past.

During college, Jo thrived academically and socially. She married her college boyfriend, **Tim**, and both entered law school together. Unfortunately, once they were outside of the "ivory tower" of college, things changed, as they faced the tough adjustments to married life and law school. They argued about everything, from big topics to little ones— when to start a family; who should cook and who should clean. After postponing having a family until after law school, Jo tried to get pregnant but could not. After three years of fertility treatment, she got pregnant, but miscarried. Tim had had enough. He moved out and filed for divorce leaving Jo devastated and angry.

After a series of destructive relationships that did not work out, Jo eventually remarried and was able to have a family after all. Her parents also had divorced, and Jo sided with her mother, remaining estranged from her father. He remarried a highly religious woman and joined her strict church. When Jo was expecting her first child, her father (with the encouragement of the second wife) sent a baby gift and offered to pay a helper to be with Jo during the first month of the baby's life. This unexpected generosity took Jo totally by surprise. To her credit, she was able to muster up the courage to call her father for the first time in years in order to thank him. She could see the influence of the second wife. Her father had become a different person. He had been truly reborn. His anger had dissipated, leaving a wiser and more tolerant old man. Jo discovered that he had a good sense of humor, and he adored Jo's children. Slowly, over the next 15 years, they reworked their relationship, even though they never talked about it.

From the perspective of an adult, Jo began to see her parents in a different light. On the one hand, her mother remained bitter about the marriage, never remarried, and pressured the children to choose sides. As the bitter root grew in Jo's mother's life, she became increasingly narrow in her interests and friendships. Her anger alienated her friends, who slowly exited her life. Jo's father, however, had sought forgiveness in his own life. He had long ago apologized to Jo's mother. She rebuffed his apology, but his new spiritual attitude permitted him to accept the rejection without bitterness. Jo saw that once he was out from under the pressures of an unhappy marriage, work, and responsibility for six children, her father could relax and reveal his tender side.

Jo had counseling, which gave her insight into her family dynamics and helped her to see how her resentment toward her father had colored her relationships with men. Over time, she also made some startling discoveries. Her first marriage had born a striking resemblance to that of her parents'—anger and control battles being themes. Her dating relationships and her second marriage had also had the same types of problems. That marriage had survived because of communication and commitment, but working on forgiveness toward her father had also changed Jo into a more tolerant and loving wife.

By the time of her father's death, Jo had totally forgiven him. Love had replaced the bitterness, anger, and estrangement. Years later, she told a friend, "It took many years to forgive my father. I am lucky that his second wife had the wisdom, courage, and compassion to risk intervening, because I was a pretty angry person. They could have just written me off. I will always be grateful to her for taking that chance with me. Forgiving Dad changed everything in my life, but I was amazed to see that as he and I made a new relationship, my marriage also improved. Somehow my issues with men got resolved in the process. We had some good times together, and my children have only good memories of their Granddad. My mother and siblings did not fare so well. They never forgave Dad, and I think the chaos of their lives resulted largely from this. My mother died a bitter, lonely old woman afflicted with Alzheimer's and mental illness. My siblings divorced multiple times and developed alcohol problems. Their kids never knew Dad. It was all so sad."

✳ Tools:

1. Sometimes we have to forgive someone over and over again before it really takes hold. Try to work on it, until the bitter root is gone. Forgiveness is one of the hardest things you will ever have to do. It will require all of your spiritual resources to accomplish. If you try but the task is overwhelming, don't hesitate to get counseling; it can help. A grudge is like cancer. Don't let it metastasize and destroy your emotional life.

2. If you cannot engage the other person in the forgiveness process—maybe they are unreceptive or even have passed away — work on this within yourself. It will still have its magical effect on you.

"ON ONE HAND"—Thanking Those Who Have Helped

Here's a story from my life — in fact, three stories that may illustrate why some personal connections remain significant even if they have been left behind for many years. The stories also show why it's important to remember and acknowledge those who make a difference in our lives.

In high school, oratory was my extracurricular activity. I had a speech teacher, Mr. Caldwell, who worked with me and helped me to win competitions on the state, national, and international levels. He always traveled with my parents to support me in these events. I graduated from high school and went on to college, graduate and medical school, losing touch with him. At my 40th high school reunion, I asked if anyone knew of his whereabouts, as years ago, I had tried to find him without success. I learned that he had died 15 years before. I still regret that I did not have a chance to thank him properly for the important role he had had in my life.

The second and third stories are about my mother. When my mother was age 92, she told me that she had seen her name in the local newspaper. Her favorite student, Benjamin Grayson, had been featured in an article describing a recent convention of entrepreneurs in technology. The billionaire honoree, Mr. Grayson, had told the audience of 400 that he owed his success to his high school teacher, Mrs. Long – my mother. She had encouraged him to enter the Alabama State Fair, the first prize (which he won) being a summer internship working under Wernher von Braun in Huntsville. This contact had changed his life, resulting in a cascading series of business and financial successes that established his company and brought thousands of jobs to his community. I contacted the reporter and asked if Mr. Grayson had known that my mother was alive. It turned out that Mr. Grayson had thought that she had long ago passed away. I arranged a meeting, in which teacher and student had a joyous reunion. At the convention the next year, Mr. Grayson invited my mother and recognized her in front of the audience. Mother's hearing was not so good at age 93, and when the audience rose to give her a standing ovation, she also clapped, assuming it was for her student. "It's for you, mother," I said. A photo of the moment caught the reserved but grateful Benjamin Grayson with a tear in his eyes. He wrote to thank me for facilitating this reunion. A year later, he was dead. His wife told me that reconnecting with my mother had been one of the most important events of his life.

Here's mother's other story. She was a tenth-generation Tennessean and proud of her Southern heritage. In 1938, she was a student at the University of Chicago. There she became engaged to a young man from Minnesota named Ollie Lundquist. The next year, she took a summer teaching position in Enterprise, Alabama, where she met my father, a charismatic Alabama country boy, with whom she fell in love. Back in school after the summer, she broke up with Ollie.

Before she died at age 94, she told me about a letter that she had written to Ollie 35 years before, after she had been diagnosed with colon cancer. In the letter, she had told him about how her life had turned out and inquired about his. She must have expressed some regret about her behavior all those years ago, as his letter said, "My life turned out very satisfactorily. I returned to Minnesota, married a woman of Norwegian descent, started my own company, and reared four good children. Do not worry about our parting. Your Southern ancestry and cultural background might have been a problem for us anyway."

I asked my mother why she had written to Ollie so many years after their breakup. She replied, "In life, there are very few people that mean something to you. You can only count them on one hand. For me, he was one."

Many people come into and out of your life. Only a few will have a real impact. If you feel down, remember those who have helped you along the way. Take a moment to thank them, and tend to this before it is too late. This will lift up both you and them, and you will always be glad you did.

- *Chapter Seven* -

SISYPHUS and the PROBLEM
of
"ROWING UPSTREAM"

In ancient Greek mythology, King Sisyphus offended Zeus by his arrogance, violence, greed, and deceit. For his sins, Zeus punished him by forcing him to push a boulder up a hill, only to have it fall down, requiring that he start all over again. The myth of Sisyphus represents the archetypal or universal human experience of frustration and futility. We often talk about this kind of experience as being that of "rowing upstream."

Have you ever felt this way about a situation, relationship, or endeavor? You try and try to make a relationship work out, but it never really succeeds. You put in an enormous amount of work

160

into a certain academic pathway, such as pre-med, only to find that you really do not enjoy the courses and your efforts produce only average results. This happened to Nick, the depressed college freshman whose story is told in Chapter 3. Maybe you, too, have become Sisyphus in this obsessive pursuit. What can you do?

Leave Sisyphus to his rock! Here's a different way to handle that boulder. A little fish is swimming in a stream. He encounters a rock but does not injure himself or waste his time and effort trying to move it. He simply swims around it.

If the obstacle is a relationship, think of the parable of the King's Wedding Feast, a piece of great wisdom from the Christian religion. The King was hosting a grand wedding feast for his son. He invited many, but when the banquet was ready, they all refused to come, choosing instead, to go about their daily business. This infuriated the King, who had spared no expense to make this a special occasion to be shared with his friends. Although disappointed by this rejection, the King recognized that those that he had invited were unworthy of the honor. He did not waste any further effort trying to convince them to come. Instead, he instructed his servants to open the doors to everyone off the street—good and bad. The banquet hall became filled with regular people who not only responded to his invitation, but also felt honored and grateful to be included. There was only one man who was not "clothed properly." Unlike all the others, who put on their best clothes as a sign of respect for the occasion and the King, this man did not even dress up! The King dealt as harshly with him as he had with those who had refused his invitation, because he, too, had proved unworthy.

Maybe you have felt this way about a relationship. You have worked hard, extending the best of yourself to another who offers little, if anything, in return. You want to share the joy of a success, or maybe you extend an offer of friendship, but they just do not respond. Instead of resonating with you, they prefer to go about their business in life—indifferent to the precious invitation you have given. If all your effort is yielding such disappointing results, it could be a signal that this relationship is not the right one for you. Open your mind to others, and respond to those who respond to you!

The same thing applies if the rock you are endlessly carrying uphill is a career goal. If you feel trapped in a never-ending cycle of little return for great effort, maybe a change is worth considering. After all, your life's work should be something that feels enjoyable and manageable given your abilities, interests, and priorities, rather than a heavy burden that you feel you must bear because you are emotionally chained to some kind of obligation. Maybe it is time to revisit your choice of a career.

Is there a big problem that you have repeatedly failed to solve no matter what approach you took? You are exhausted and have run out of options. Rather than continuing to "row upstream," *stop* and mentally allow yourself to "go with the flow." Allow some time and space for other solutions to emerge. There may be a different answer that you never considered before. Or a change occurs in your life that makes you think differently about the situation, and it does not even matter anymore. If, in the end, you cannot solve a problem, the wisest course of action may be simply to leave it unsolved, knowing that you have done your best, and move on to something new. Time may take care of it in a way we cannot predict.

✗ Tools:

1. What if you cannot give up what you are doing even though it is frustrating? You may feel that you have to try and try again to make something work out, even though each time seems to fail. Go easy on yourself if this happens to you. There are lessons to be learned with each failure.

2. The process of "letting go" can be like trying to stop smoking. Some smokers start and stop and start again many times before they quit for the last time. Research has shown that it can take many trials before the smoker succeeds in quit-

ting, so keep trying to understand what is keeping you emotionally engaged in a frustrating situation or relationship. When you are ready, you will walk away from the boulder and move on with your life.

- *Chapter Eight* -

The MIRACLE OF HEALING

Life is full of happiness and disappointment. People let us down. We make mistakes. We do not get something that we greatly desire. We flub an exam. We are passed over for a prize or a promotion. We let others down. We destroy a relationship because we do not communicate our needs or problems directly, or we act out our anger, jealousy, or pride. We try to make amends, but to no avail. We are left with regret, shame, guilt, or anger. We are engulfed with hopelessness that we can ever be healed of the hurt. Friends try to reassure us that we will get over it, but we don't believe them. The hurt lingers for what feels like a long, long time.

Time goes by, and years later, we realize that a transformation has occurred. We are no longer endlessly suffering under the burden of raw emotions. We think of the painful situation or person without automatically spinning into a tidal wave of old feelings. We realize we are finally over it. We have healed, but we have no idea how it occurred.

"Time heals" is true. We don't understand how it happens, but here is what we know.

Healing comes when we know we have closed one chapter in our lives and have entered another. Charles Dederich came up with a saying that became the ultimate street wisdom of the 1960s:

Today is the First Day of the Rest of Your Life!

You know you have healed when you have reached a kind of *emotional neutrality* about the issue or event. We have developed a new narrative about a situation and have attached to it a new emotional meaning that enables us to replace pain with feelings of neutrality or even indifference. It takes some work to get to this place. Maybe we have talked about it with a friend or counselor who has listened with the neutrality we need. Maybe we have discussed it only with ourselves, reworking it over time emotionally. Maybe we have just cried until we have wrung all of the painful feelings out of the experience leaving only the desiccated remains to be shelved in the storage room (the unconscious) of our minds. There it can remain for the rest of our lives without disturbing us. We might forget about it over time, and that's okay, or we might take it off the shelf sometime if we want, but either way, the feelings around it are no longer flooding our emotional lives—interfering with our relationships and our sense of self-worth. How do you work on healing?

Tools:

1. Journaling may be useful in getting a new narrative down on paper and working with it.

2. Record your dreams in a dream journal. Don't have any dreams? If you put a notebook and pen by your bed and jot down any dream fragment you get, you may be surprised to find yourself recording dreams in vivid sequences. Once you have a connection going with your dream world, you can begin to pose questions to yourself before you go to sleep. If you do, make sure that your question is specific and unambiguous, so that the meaning of your dream response is clear. Believe it or not, your dream world can tap into a universe of wisdom that can be both comforting and instructive. Once you tap into this, you might be amazed by the profound insights you gain about a problem—wisdom given by your own soul. Here is a story of how dreams

helped someone overcome an emotional obstacle and discern the truth about a relationship:

Anika, a college student, was involved in a tumultuous relationship with **Terrence**. She tried hard to make the relationship work, but it seemed that problems were always arising.

She began working with her dreams. One night she posed the ultimate question to herself: "If I marry Terrence, what will life be like?" Her dream that night was as follows: She and Terrence were at a crowded party given at her house by someone she did not know. She did not know anyone there. The scene was chaotic—people were knocking over furniture and getting into fights. She felt afraid and fled the scene.

The next night, Anika asked herself the opposite question: "If I do not marry Terrence, what will life be like?" In her dream that night, she was sitting beside a tranquil lake. The feeling tone of the dream was calm, and she was content.

Anika did not like the unmistakable messages conveyed by the dreams. She had hoped her dreams would tell her that the relationship would work, but what they gave her was the opposite. She could not miss the "sting of truth" played out in the dreams' stories. As difficult as it was initially for her to confront the reality she had defensively denied, she used the wisdom of the dreams to work through her feelings about Terrence and the meaning the relationship had for her.

The dreams helped Anika sort through some complicated issues left over from her childhood. Through counseling, she began to see that Terrence reminded her of her father, whom she saw as an authoritarian, critical man she could never please. She wanted to be accepted by Terrence in a way she did not feel accepted by her father. As she realized the overlap between her feelings about Terrence and those about her father, she began to see that she was trying to rework that relationship through Terrence.

But Terrence was not her father, and she needed to separate the two relationships emotionally. She worked on understanding how her feelings about her father permeated her perceptions of and reactions to Terrence. She began to see Terrence as a separate man, different from her father. It was not his responsibility to rescue her from the unhappiness lingering from her relationship with her father.

At the same time, she saw that she was not particularly comfortable with Terrence's ability to listen and communicate about their differences. As she grew to accept reality, the truth of the dreams comforted her, allowing her to disengage gradually from the relationship. Gradually she developed a healing narrative. "I got into a destructive relationship. In spite of the pain, I stayed in it way too long, because I had to work out an issue left over from the past. When we finally broke up, I was relieved." The dreams had helped awaken her to the truth. As she worked through the issues, she often thought

170

of the dreams that had challenged, comforted, and educated her, helping her to confront an uncomfortable reality, make a tough decision, and heal. In the healing process, she was able to develop both an understanding of the experience, and along with it, a narrative with new emotional meaning and feeling of neutrality.

Endowing a healing narrative with *emotional meaning* takes time, and, unfortunately, there is no way to short-circuit the process. You may think that you are over a problem but, like the bleeding that happens when you remove a surgical bandage too soon, you may relapse into grief and anger. Be patient and continue to work on it. Processing the experience over time with all of the associated emotions will help you to understand and learn from it. When you have healed, you will know it. You will have the narrative and the meaning. Then the chapter will be closed, and you will truly be ready to move on.

✗ Tools: While you are trying to heal:

1. Find something that nurtures your soul—family, friends, hobbies, nature, art, music, cooking, animals, whatever. Engage in the activity as much as you can—at least weekly.

2. Develop a social support system — a group of friends or family members whom you can count on for companionship, sympathy, and honest advice. Then make those relationships reciprocal. Be there for them too.

3. Give counseling a try if you are struggling. What do you have to lose?

4. Keep your expectations of yourself and others reasonable.

5. When others sabotage your good works, try to disengage with humor. After all, "No good deed goes unpunished!" When others do harm to you, remember that "Time wounds all heels."

6. Turn outward rather than inward. When you feel able, find a way to serve others. As we found in the Super Strategies Chapter 6, giving to others in need takes us out of our own pain and enriches our soul.

7. Take a moment from whatever you are doing, take a breath, and enjoy life. Admire a beautiful snowfall, sunrise or sunset, a flower, fall colors, the song of a bird, a good joke, the joy of being with a friend, the inspiration you get from a teacher. You only go around once, and life passes in the blink of an eye. Don't miss the little joys along the way.

- *Chapter Nine* -

SYNCHRONICITY

When **Joan** was a first-year graduate student, she was mentored by a particular faculty member who had sponsored her and named her to receive the fellowship that funded her years there. During the summer before her second year, he died of a chronic illness. When he died, the department decided to change its direction and phase out of Joan's area of interest. The only other student in her area, regrettably, flunked out of the program, leaving Joan alone and without a mentor.

That fall, Joan encountered the department chair in a hallway, where he was standing with a middle-aged man she didn't know. The chair expressed regret about her mentor's death and then introduced Joan to his companion, a visiting professor from a distinguished European university and the world's authority in an area closely related to Joan's. He was to be on the campus for the year. The chair added that it was regrettable that the department would no longer sponsor Joan's academic area of interest, "but perhaps John can help you." He then turned to the visitor and said, "John, I'm sure you don't mind teaching Edgar's courses" — the two large survey courses Joan's late mentor had taught, usually attended by at least 300 students each. After the chair walked away, the professor turned to Joan, looking quite upset. "I was supposed to tutor a couple of graduate students but otherwise have no teaching obligations, so that I could write the second edition of my book," he said. "What am I going to do now?" Joan told him that she would help. He appointed her head teaching fellow for both courses. She would supervise the teaching fellows, who taught the smaller groups and read and graded papers. Rummaging through her late mentor's notes, Joan put together a list of topics. With that list, her new mentor was knowledgeable enough to deliver his lectures extemporaneously — and well enough that he received standing ovations when his classes concluded.

Joan could not have predicted on the day of that unplanned hallway meeting how much it would impact her life. Later, John took her under his wing as she wrote her dissertation. He chaired her dissertation committee and went out of his way to tutor her in person. Back at his home university, five years after Joan's degree was awarded, he arranged for her to do a post-doctoral research fellowship, giving her a valuable opportunity to experi-

175

ence life in a European university setting. Until his death in his 80s, they continued to correspond and to visit in person, sharing a long and supportive companionship. When he died, she and many other of his students from around the world gathered with his family and colleagues to pay tribute to him.

In hindsight, that fortuitous meeting was an example of *synchronicity,* a term coined by Carl Jung. In plain words, synchronicity is a *miraculous coincidence*, the significance of which is rarely appreciated until well after it occurs. This series of coincidences — the death of Joan's prior professor, her new mentor's sabbatical the following fall, his unexpected assignment to teach Edgar's courses, his surprise and anxiety about this unexpected task, and Joan's willingness to overcome her own sense of inadequacy to respond to the need of a guest from abroad — combined to create a unique and lifelong friendship.

Synchronicity is happening all of the time if you tune into it. You are late to a meeting and just *happen* to find a car pulling out of the one available parking place in the lot. An old friend you have not thought about for 20 years just *happens* to call you at that moment. You have lost your job. A friend invites you to a party where you just *happen* to meet someone who just that day lost an employee with exactly your set of skills. Spring break is coming, and at the last minute, you can't get a flight to Florida, so instead, you decide on impulse to go to the Bahamas with a friend. You schedule a tennis match, which is rained out, so you and your friend decide to go to a movie, where a mother begins to scream that her child is choking on a gumball. You perform a Heimlich maneuver (learn what this is!) that saves the child's life. Coincidence? So let's run through this sequence again: Flights to Florida *just happened* to be full, so you *just happened* to take your vacation in the Bahamas. You just *happened* to go to *that particular movie* on *that particular day* at *that location* at *that particular showing*—all because it *just happened* to rain and your tennis game was canceled. As a result of this, a life was saved. What are the odds of that?

✗ Tools:

1. Look for the miracles in life. If synchronicity gives you an opportunity to experience something unique or develop a new friendship, do not pass it by, even if you feel scared and ill-prepared. It could be a life-changing experience.

2. Also watch for opportunities to help others. Synchronicity may permit you to change their lives. You may even have a chance to assume the role of a guardian angel, someone who intervenes in some uniquely fortuitous way that helps another. Remember John's aneurysm? Was it just

coincidence that he had been going out with a young woman whom I knew, and that she happened to mention his headaches to me? I did not expect or plan that event, but for this one moment, I was given the opportunity to help. For this one occasion I was John's guardian angel, and so was the student who saved the child's life in that movie theater.

- *Chapter Ten* -

The "STUMBLES" OF LIFE

INDEPENDENCE and "CULTURE SHOCK"

All of the preceding chapters have dealt with different aspects of the Transition. This is a wonderful time of growth and self-discovery, as you think about life and explore the potential it holds. Most young people do just fine. Although everyone makes mistakes, usually they don't create too much havoc in our lives. But sometimes, course corrections are needed, as Kaitlin and Ken discovered.

Kaitlin was the first in her devoutly religious Midwest family to go to college. The small town in which she grew up was stable. Nobody moved in or out, families stayed intact, and everyone attended the same church. If anyone had problems, the community knew about it and responded. When Kaitlin left to attend a large university in California, it was not what she had expected. Her freshman class was larger in size than her home town, and everyone was different. Her roommates were from Los Angeles, New York, Philadelphia, and Chicago. They did not hold strong religious beliefs, and they knew about things that Kaitlin had never thought about —alcohol, drugs, sex, gangs, violence in the community, and Philadelphia's "Social Register." There were no curfews and no parents waiting up until she came home from a date. No one told her where she could and couldn't go or with whom she could "hang out." She could go to class or skip it. She could sleep in on Sunday and not go to church. With so much freedom and so many lifestyles to sample—where to begin?!

Freshman year for Kaitlin was a year of wild experimentation. She stepped out of everything she knew from back home and put the "pedal to the metal" in life—sex, alcohol, marijuana, and all night parties. All of this took a toll. She developed a STD (sexually-transmitted disease), and things did not go well in her courses. She ended up on academic probation but found it hard to re-engage in her classes. The Dean suggested she take some time off, and she returned home, where her family suggested she get a job. After working for three years, she decided to transfer to her state school, where she finished college in four years. "It just wasn't right for me," she said later about her initial university experience. "The culture shock was too great, and I had no idea how to handle it."

Ken entered a west coast college on an R.O.T.C. scholarship. He was proud to be from an old Southern family with a tradition of military service dating back to Colonial days. Men from every generation of his ancestors had served in the military, and a first cousin, continuing the tradition, was serving in Afghanistan as a colonel in the Army. Ken had also been accepted at one of the military academies, where his father, who was an Army general, had studied. Ken planned to enter the military but decided to try a different college experience.

In college, though, he found himself in a totally different environment than he expected. His military training courses, held off-campus, had only six students, and those were from other colleges in the area as well as Ken's. On his campus, he found that his pro-military views were not popular, and his plan to make a career in the military raised eyebrows among his classmates. Freshman year was not an easy adjustment. Ken felt isolated and became increasingly quiet about his commitment to the military. Except for his military classmates and a few old friends from back home, he felt there was no one else who could relate to him. He became increasingly uncomfortable with what he considered to be a lack of structure, discipline, respect, and morality in the campus community. Despite those feelings, he focused on his classes and did well. However, at the end of his freshman year, he announced on his social networking wall posting that he had again been accepted to a military academy and would be entering the next fall as a freshman. Reflecting later on his college experience, he said, "I was really naïve. It was really culture shock. I had no idea that people opposed the military, and that those who supported it were considered 'weird.' But I don't feel that I made a mistake. I had been pretty sheltered in my upbringing. That year taught me a lot about myself and the world. Exposing myself to others who were 180 degrees out from what I was used to helped me define who I really was. It was a lonely time, but it taught me that serving my country in the military was really important to me."

Three years later at the commissioning ceremony for Ken's original military training classmates, one of them, **Peter**, discussed his college experience. He agreed that it had been "kind of rough going the military route" in that campus climate, but his response had been quite different from Ken's: "The College had other advantages, and I learned to deflect rude comments with humor. I figured that college was life. This was my choice, and others could make different ones. I didn't let them push my buttons. People really didn't care, as long as I did not have a chip on my shoulder about it. I found out that I had a lot of other things in common with people, especially sports."

The college environment can provide much more freedom than most young people knew at home. Sometimes that freedom can be a heady experience that can be hard to handle. Other contrasts between the home and college environments can be very stark, too. Familiar, comfortable routines and people are not around. Many of the people you meet come from places and backgrounds very different from yours. Their styles may be pleasant and easy to get along with or difficult and abrasive. You may find yourself asking why you are here and whether coming was a big mistake. You may feel overwhelmed, homesick, lonely, scared, and inadequate.

Before you panic, take a deep breath and consider this. Yes, like Kaitlin and Ken, maybe you will decide you did make a mistake and want to leave. But first, try letting someone know before you "jump ship," and think about giving yourself more of a chance to adjust. If you are homesick, remember that your home is still inside you even though you are physically in a new place. Your anxiety may subside as you develop friends and a new life routine. If home was a place you were glad to leave, you now have a chance to make a different, more satisfying life, as you come to terms with your old one. It may take some time to make friends and find "kindred spirits," but maybe, like Peter, you will find people who share your interests or engage you in new ones. If you find your buttons are being pushed, see if you can detach a bit from the swirling emotions and figure out what is pushing them. Then, work on deactivating the switch so that you do not overreact. Challenges to your ideas and your characteristic reactions can even be a valuable experience if they help you learn ways to handle such situations in the future.

Most students grow into the freedom of this stage in life and handle it without serious problems. Like Kaitlin and Ken, they can course-correct and learn from mistakes. Some, however, have more difficulty, lashing out toward *others* through bullying or hazing, or directing anger toward *themselves* through self-destructive behaviors, like drinking, bingeing or starving, using drugs, or destructive sexual, aggressive, or other behavior. This section will be like the highway warning signs alerting us to "Dangers Up Ahead." A timely notice is all most of us need!

HARMING OTHERS – Bullying and Hazing

Bullying and hazing are related problems of inappropriate aggression. They involve inflicting harm or pain on others. Bullying is seen in young children and continues to adulthood. In earlier years, it can involve aggressive and demeaning remarks and/or direct physical acts of aggression, but later, bullying often becomes indirect and verbal. We talked about the destructive effects of cyber bullying, a form of harassment. Sarcasm and put-downs are verbal forms of aggression. Also inappropriate are hostile comments and behaviors that disparage others because of sex, ethnic group, religion, sexual orientation, or any other characteristic that sets someone apart from the majority. Bullying is about power and control, and whether the aggression stems from poorly managed anger or low self-esteem, it is inappropriate and, in some cases, illegal.

Hazing is bullying that occurs within the context of an initiation or membership rite. Such traditions, which provide rituals for

accepting new members into a community, have deep psychological roots within the human psyche. In America, most
organizations and clubs have ceremonies for new members,
while most religions have well-known rites, such as confirmation
for most Christian denominations, and the bar or bat mitzvah for
Jews. In most cases, induction ceremonies are positive ways to
celebrate inclusion of others while uniting the community in a
common purpose.

Hazing typically occurs in fraternities, sororities, and college
clubs and, at times, in military units or sports teams. It can start
off as an innocent requirement that initiates complete a task for
membership. But sometimes, the demands can be like the
Twelve Labors of Hercules. The tasks can be severe, distorting
the ancient psychological principle with an unreasonable obstacle that must be overcome.

While trying to comply, initiates may be physically stressed or
injured, harassed, or humiliated. In some cases, initiators do not
intend harm, but as in a prank gone wrong, things spin out of
control and result in injury or even death. In other cases, initiation rites are deliberate ways to legitimize Shadow qualities of
power and control. Initiators rationalize their demands that new
members prove their worthiness for inclusion into the group.
They can establish any rules they want, and the more extreme
the rules, the greater their sense of power. And, although you
would think that those who suffered the most when they were

going through the initiation rights would be the ones to inflict maximum misery, in many cases, it is the opposite. Those who suffered the least may mete out the most severe punishment.

How do these ideas become the norm for the group? In deciding what initiates must do, leaders may dominate discussions to such a degree that others, under peer pressure, are reluctant to object to what they recognize is wrong. Remember how most people go along with the "collective unconscious"? This is what can happen here, with members rationalizing their silence by thinking that the probability of real harm is small. They tell themselves that maybe the demand is "pushing the limits" but after all, others have gone through it and survived. They deny or minimize the reality that extreme physical and/or psychological tasks can result in significant physical and/or psychological injury or even death. Stories describe fatal instances in which young people were beaten, forced to spend the night in freezing temperatures or endure sleep deprivation, locked in a car trunk for extended lengths of time, or required to drink massive amounts of alcohol, gallons of water, or bottles of Tabasco. Some are even required to inflict wounds on themselves. In some tragic cases, initiates are taunted to the point of suicide. Hazing can become the herd mentality gone amok. Schools have banned it, and in most states, hazing is illegal, but problems continue.

Why do initiates tolerate what they know to be physical and/or emotional abuse? For some, there is such a strong need to belong to the collective group that they will do whatever is asked despite the risks to their health or lives. They accept the power differential and tell themselves that as subordinates, they must comply with the demands of their superiors. For others, it is much like climbing Mt. Everest; they want to rise to the challenge. They deny the dangers and roll the dice, in some cases with disastrous results.

✷ Tool:

If it feels bad, either physically or emotionally, it is bad, at least for you. You do not have to go along with the program. Stop and consider if you are comfortable with what the collective is doing. If you have mixed feelings about it, talk it over with a neutral friend, parent, teacher, minister or rabbi, counselor, or physician. They can be an objective sounding board to give you perspective. They can also intervene to set limits on a situation that could be lethal, either for you or someone else.

HARMING YOURSELF

Alcohol

Alcohol is one of the most common problems in America, especially for youth. The most recent Youth Risk Behavior Survey conducted by the U.S. Centers for Disease Control and Prevention[1] (CDC) reported that nearly three-quarters of students (72.5 percent) have tried alcohol at some time, and just under one-quarter, 24.2 percent, reported having a recent episode of heavy drinking (more than five drinks over a couple of hours). This is a *sobering* statistic: *The number one cause of death for teenagers and young adults is motor vehicle accidents. For those who drink or ride with someone who has been drinking, or who fail to buckle up, the risk of dying in a motor vehicle accident is greatly elevated.*

Alcohol problems can start early. Some young people learn to associate "partying" with drinking. They soon find that the only way they can "relax" is by drinking. Others try to "drown their sorrows" in a few drinks. It is easy to progress from having one drink, to having a few, to drinking habitually in order to ease "withdrawal" symptoms the next morning. Before you know it, you are caught in a vicious downward cycle, and you have a major alcohol problem. What would this mean for you?

---

[1] Centers for Disease Control and Prevention. Youth Risk Behavior Surveillance — United States, 2009. Surveillance Summaries, June 4, 2010. MMWR 2010; 59 (No. SS-5): pp 73, 75, 77

Alcohol abuse can lead to negative consequences, including inappropriate aggression, mental disorders such as depression and anxiety, and relationship problems. It can also cause some types of cancers and other medical disorders involving the brain, liver, and heart, to name a few. Also, alcohol weakens inhibitions. You may say and do things when you drink that you would not say or do when you are sober—like make inappropriate sexual or aggressive remarks or act in ways that you later regret. As a medical school professor once observed *the human conscience is soluble in alcohol*, so your ethical standards are apt to dissolve "under the influence."

What if you continue to drink and develop a problem? You really have only two options—get help for the problem or deal with the negative consequences mentioned above. Since alcohol dependence is a chronic medical disorder, to get on top of the problem requires a life-long commitment to sobriety and ongoing support from others struggling with the same commitment. Not addressing the problem is worse. Is this a problem you need?

✷ Tools:

1. Think choice. You actually have one and, as with smoking, many youths decide not to drink. They find that you really don't need alcohol to have a great time at a party. In fact, parties are more fun

189

if you can talk to others coherently and not say or do foolish things. They also find that getting "wasted" feels awful, especially the next day. If you're already feeling down or stressed out, alcohol will only make things worse. Not drinking need not make you a social misfit. At parties, grab a soda or glass of club soda with a lemon or lime. Focus on good conversation, music, and dancing, rather than the food or drink. Meet new people or get to know someone better.

P.S. Alcohol packs a lot of empty calories!

2. If you drink or are planning to start, drink moderately. What is moderate drinking? Opinions vary, but according to the Dietary Guidelines for Americans established by the U.S. Department of Agriculture, it is no more than one drink a day for women or two drinks for men. One drink is defined as 1.5 ounces of spirits (such as gin or bourbon), a 12-ounce can or bottle of beer, or one five-ounce glass of wine.

3. Think of traffic lights when you drink. No alcohol is represented by a green light that tells you

"go" — that is, your road is clear and safe. One drink turns on a yellow light that means "caution," and after two drinks a red light flashes signaling you to stop.

4. If you think drinking might be getting to be a problem, it probably is. Test yourself—give up alcohol altogether for six months. If you cannot do it, you have a problem. Take the **CAGE**, a good online screening tool for alcohol dependence. If you answer any of these in the affirmative, you may have a problem. The acronym comes from this list of questions:

Have you ever felt:

A need to **C**ut down on your drinking?
Annoyed when others criticize your drinking?
Guilty about your drinking?
A need for an **E**ye-opener in the morning?

5. If you think a friend has a drinking problem, talk to him or her. Don't be surprised if someone protests loudly and denies having a problem.

191

Denial is common in alcohol problems. Get the person to take the **CAGE**, or suggest going together to see an advisor or counselor.

6. Alcoholics Anonymous ("A.A."), a 12 Step Group approach to alcohol problems, has been proven to be an effective way for adults and teens to get and stay sober. Check out their links to online pamplets: "A Message to Teenagers–How to tell when drinking is becoming a problem" and "Young People and A.A."

www.aa.org

7. Teen Anon offers help for teens with a drinking or drug problem or for those who love them. Although it uses a 12 Step approach like A.A., it is not affiliated with them:

http://www.teen-anon.com/home.htm

8. The National Institute on Drug Abuse (NIDA) and the National Institute on Alcohol Abuse and

Alcoholism (NIAAA) are components of the National Institute of Health. They have pamphlets full of information on alcohol and drug abuse and links for teens, college students, and adults:

http://www.drugabuse.gov/nidahome.html

http://www.thecoolspot.gov

Weight and Eating Disorders

Eating is one of life's greatest pleasures, but most people struggle with weight, either keeping it off or keeping it on. Weight affects our body image and self-confidence, as it is part of the face or appearance we present to the world. Stress can affect our eating habits and weight in a big way; some overeat, while others lose their appetites. In addition, for young women, monthly hormonal fluctuations can result in discouraging weight gains as well as mood changes.

For both sexes, weight can be a major life issue, often aggravated by a cultural landscape full of celebrities whose images foster unrealistic and perfectionistic physical standards that even they cannot maintain! Some people get into yo-yo cycles of dieting and weight loss followed by a return to their usual eating habits and weight gain. Since the body triggers all sorts of starvation responses to dieting, the weight comes back on with extra to boot. Women, in particular, seem prone to feel stressed about weight. In addition to dieting, some turn to extreme measures, such as excessive exercise, severe calorie limitations, or even starvation (anorexia) or bingeing and purging (bulimia).

Colleges and universities are taking these problems seriously. Increasingly, colleges are requiring that entering freshmen submit a Body Mass Index (BMI) as a part of their pre-requisite physical exam. Those who do not provide this cannot matriculate. If there is a student whose BMI is borderline low, they may be required to sign an agreement to be monitored frequently and maintain their weight within certain parameters.

⚒ Tools:

1. Get comfortable with your body and accept that a big component of your basic physical constitution is genetically ordained. The only part you can really impact is environmental; that means calorie intake and physical activity. If you are predisposed to being overweight due to genes and want to maintain a weight below what your genes dictate, you may always struggle with this issue.

2. Figure out your "set point," a reasonable baseline weight that permits you to function with adequate energy but avoids the health risks associated with being significantly overweight (like elevated blood pressure, cholesterol, heart disease, overweight-related diabetes) or underweight (loss of menstrual periods, endocrine abnormalities, osteoporosis). Note that research has suggested that for some people, 10 pounds over what has been called ideal in the past is associated with good health. Whatever weight you decide, try to maintain it plus or minus a few pounds. When over or under this weight, adjust your intake or exercise to return to baseline.

3. If you struggle with being overweight, check out the following program:

Take Off Pounds Sensibly (**www.tops.org**)

4. Find ways to relieve stress without overeating. This book gives some tools for stress management (See, for example, the Anxiety section in Chapter 5—Emotional Suffering).

5. Learn to enjoy the total experience of eating, especially the companionship of others. Focus on conversation, rather than food. If at a party or buffet, station yourself on the other side of the room away from the food and limit calorie-laden drinks, especially alcohol.

6. Watch out for complex carbohydrates—i.e., starches like bread, pasta, rice, potatoes, and chips. In some people, such foods can produce blood sugar cycles in which they feel full then voraciously hungry. Go easy at parties. Snacks, in conjunction with alcohol, can really pack on the pounds.

7. As the Greek philosopher Aristotle advised, **seek moderation in all things.** If anxious about your eating, remember there will always be another meal, so slow down and relax. Aim for portion control and balance and try not to obsess about food and your weight. Remember that the *physical dimension is just* one of four compass points of life (see Chapter 4), so re-balance your focus to include the other three.

8. If you find yourself trying any of the extreme measures mentioned above, like starving or bingeing, don't fool yourself into thinking that all is okay. You are subjecting your body to unhealthy stress that can have long-term serious health consequences. Now is the time to understand what weight means to you emotionally and get a healthier approach to this life-long challenge. Are you a perfectionist? If so, how did you get to be that way and why? Is it tied to fear of rejection or abandonment by others? Here's a thought: Dare to be normal, not perfect! No one is perfect anyway, so chasing it is an illusion. See yourself as a total person—not just a number on a bathroom scale. If we get ill or are under duress, maybe we will gain or lose a large amount of weight, but inside we are still the same person. Those who truly care for us accept us, weight and all. Show yourself the same love and acceptance.

9. If you are into the habit of bingeing and purging, over-exercising, or starving, and cannot seem to get a handle on it, see this as a symptom of a

deeper issue that needs to be addressed and soon. Sometimes once the bingeing, purging, starving, or over-exercising is controlled, an underlying clinical depression or anxiety disorder emerges. Get help from the counseling center, family doctor, or mental health professional to address the symptoms as well as underlying emotional issues. If out of control, don't delay. Get help before permanent health damage or even death occur. As the death of singer Karen Carpenter sadly illustrates, anorexia is a tenacious disease that may become chronic. Its ravages on the body can be fatal.

10. There are many resources for help with eating disorders. Here is the National Eating Disorders website:

http://www.nationaleatingdisorders.org

Sexuality

As we talked about above with sexual identity and orientation, sexuality is a part of who we are and how we define ourselves.

It can also be a pleasurable, meaningful, and enriching part of a committed relationship. During the Transition years, as we mature physically, we may become more or less aware of sexual feelings and urges and the various options available to us. Here are some things to keep in mind as you think about sexual behavior.

✱ Tools:

1. Learn responsibility in this area of life and make choices in line with your core values.

2. Some young people are choosing to wait about sex until later, when they are more sure that the relationship is a committed one. And the latest brain research is on their side—the more turned on you are, the more turned off is your brain's ability to help you make a good decision in this area! P.S. Remember that there are ways to be close physically other than sex.

3. If you choose to become sexually involved, think safety. Take precautions to avoid sexually transmitted diseases (STDs) and pregnancy. Find out

whether or not your partner has had an STD. The Health Service or clinic can provide non-judgmental help in this area, including HIV and other STD testing as well as birth control counseling and information. Use a condom every time.

4. Sex is more than just a physical act. It can have major emotional as well as physical consequences. Remember that there is a person wrapped around that body. Avoiding acting out sexually by being promiscuous or taking advantage of someone's attachment to you if you do not feel the same way. Using people sexually can cause harm to them and to you, and if that is all there is to the relationship, move on. If you are getting involved with someone, avoid feeling pressured to have sex, and don't allow yourself to be used. If you are uncomfortable with what is happening, stop and say so. Appreciate your internal brakes and communicate your feelings honestly. Guys, if a woman says "**No,**" that means "**NO,**" whether or not alcohol is involved, so **STOP**.

5. If alcohol is a part of the picture, things can go downhill fast. Remember the line about the conscience being soluble in alcohol? One young woman went to the emergency room in a panic when she woke up in the morning and discovered evidence in her bed that she had had sex with someone the night before. She had been drinking heavily at a party and had blacked out, so she had no memory whatsoever of the incident, much less whom her partner might have been. She had to be tested, treated, and followed medically for months. Worse, she had considerable remorse and loss of self-esteem about her lack of control, as well as anxiety about all of the unknowns of that night.

6. Women, be aware of date rape drugs. These can cause temporary "black outs" or memory impairment. Unless you are very sure of your circumstances and companions, never leave your drink unattended or drink from open or common containers. There is now an inexpensive product by Drink Safe Technologies° — testing strips that you can carry with you and use to test your drink for any of the major date rape drugs (commonly

gamma hydroxybutyrate GHB or Ketamine). You test by putting a drop of the drink on the indicator spot using a swizzle stick or even your finger and watching for a color change. Keeping some with you just in case is a good idea.

Drugs

Sometimes, as they use their new freedom to experiment in life, young people try drugs. The CDC Youth Risk Survey mentioned earlier found that among the ninth through twelfth-grade students surveyed, just under 37 percent said that they had tried marijuana at least once, and almost 21 percent said that they had used it within the 30 days before the survey was taken.

Teens may think that marijuana is benign, but they are wrong. Research is showing that it can give you memory problems, sap your motivation, and even set you up for possible major mental illness, including significant depression or worse— maybe not immediately, but often down the road. And because today's marijuana is much more potent than that of the 1960s, the damage it can do can be considerable, especially on the brain's executive function centers that are developing during the teen years. The following true story illustrates how destructive this drug can be, and its damaging effects are compounded by alcohol.

Stan began using pot and alcohol at a nationally-ranked high school but was able to make outstanding grades nonetheless. After he learned that he was a National Merit Finalist just before graduation, he dropped out of school and joined the Navy. He graduated from Boot Camp and was deployed to the Persian Gulf. He was on his way to a promotion, when he was caught with marijuana and expelled from the Navy. He returned home to live with his father. Without the structure of school or the military, he could not organize his life. He briefly worked construction but was unreliable and was fired. He continued to drink and use marijuana and became depressed. When his girlfriend broke up with him, he committed suicide. He was 19.

If using marijuana has risks, street drugs such as cocaine, "speed" (amphetamines), "club drugs" (like ecstasy), hallucinogens (e.g. LSD and mescaline), and steroids (that get athletes in trouble) are even worse. They will flat out do you *no good*, only *harm, both mentally and physically,* and they might even kill you. The same is true for illicitly distributed prescription drugs, such as tranquilizers or amphetamines that are used without a doctor's supervision for a legitimate medical reason. These drugs raise *real* problems, including legal ones that could put you in prison. Life is challenging enough. You don't need those problems!

✳ Tools:

1. If you are doing drugs, you will need a medical evaluation to check for possible medical consequences of the drug abuse.

2. You will also need ongoing help and support. Consider counseling or a group. Check out these 12 Step Self-help groups based on Alcoholics Anonymous. You will see that you are not alone:

   A. Teen-Anon: (alcohol and drugs)
      http://www.teen-anon.com/home.htm

   B. Narcotics Anonymous: (focuses on addiction)
      http://www.na.org

   C. Cocaine Anonymous: http://www.ca.org

Self-Injury

Some young people do things to injure themselves when they are depressed. This can include cutting or burning themselves as a means of inflicting self-punishment. Why do they do this?

Remember that depression produces chemical and psychological states that are highly abnormal and above all, unrealistic. As a part of this, people may feel worthless, guilty, hopeless, and helpless. They may feel like they deserve punishment. Sometimes inflicting physical pain feels like it diminishes these negative feelings, even though such behavior is counterproductive and hard to understand. If you or someone you know is inflicting self-injury, there is a better way to deal with disappointment and pain. Encourage them to get help or if it is you, take a step toward releasing yourself from this cycle. Help is available. Seek it from a doctor or mental health professional.

- *Chapter Eleven* -

KEEP YOUR EYE
ON THE PRIZE!

Aim High, Play Fair, and Smell the Roses Along the Way

Final thoughts....

❖ Be open to the *possibilities* of this time of life, and
   see it as a *fantastic journey*!

❖ Learn about your *prism* and your *style*.

❖ Turn off the "Auto Pilot," step out of the "collective
   unconscious," and seek your *individual life*.

- ❖ Find the best *"fit"*— your *archetypal* life role that is in harmony with your core being and values.

- ❖ As you progress, grow into a *"We"* perspective that makes room for others who may be *different* from you.

- ❖ Be grateful for the companionship of *friends* whom life has brought to you, for they will make the journey with you.

- ❖ Enjoy the Internet and social networking, but turn the computer off and get out with real *people*.

- ❖ Building *confidence* takes years, so just work on *self-esteem* a little at a time and protect it from forces that would erode it.

- ❖ Think about the *Big Picture* and find a philosophy, like the *four compass points*, to maintain balance.

- ❖ Remember Aristotle: *Seek moderation in all things*.

❖ Life is full of *surprises* and *changes*, some positive, some negative. View problems as *opportunities* rather than *difficulties*. As Winston Churchill said,

"Attitude is a little thing that makes a big difference."
Think positively.

❖ *Independence* means learning to manage emotions and behavior in a responsible way.

❖ When *problems* arise, remember that you have a *choice* about how you will deal with them.

❖ Become aware of your *emotions*, as your ability to manage these is essential to your happiness. Learn to recognize how your emotions feel physically and what psychological defenses come into play when you find yourself feeling stressed by painful or uncomfortable situations or people.

❖ Nothing and no one can *make* you feel either on top of the world or the opposite— ashamed, humiliated, angry, rejected, or anxious. Only you are

208

responsible for your feelings and behavior, and that's true for your partner and friends as well.

❖ See new experiences as opportunities to enlarge your *perspective*. Everyone is different. Even if you feel personally attacked or threatened by someone, try to figure out which of your buttons have been pushed and work on deactivating those buttons, so that they don't cause you to behave in ways that you will later regret.

❖ Be aware of the *Shadow*, as it is a part of us — the darker side that we have to accept as ours, rather than project it onto others. The Shadow reminds us that all humans have dark as well as light sides in their character and personalities. Pay special attention to the *Money Shadow* and do not allow it to control, diminish, or destroy your life.

❖ Enjoy the magic of *falling in love*, but if it crashes and burns, it can still teach you a lot about yourself and the ideals that you found in the other person. If you made a mistake and misjudged

209

someone, you can make a different choice the next time. Look for someone with a *deep and abiding interest in you*. Importantly, leave people with serious character flaws alone. You cannot change them, and there is little for you there except a world of hurt.

❖ See the *totality* of life. Accept the joy and pain. Work on the great achievements of adulthood: to *love* and to *work*.

❖ Accept that along with *pleasure* and fulfillment, life also brings *suffering*. Painful emotions, such as anxiety, shame, jealousy, envy, and anger, can erode your sense of well-being and harm your relationships. Talk about these feelings with a friend or counselor, so that you do not endlessly suffer under their burden.

❖ If painful feelings get to be unmanageable, or you find yourself getting sidetracked into destructive activities, get *help*. No problem is so large or so complicated that it cannot be resolved in some way.

❖ If someone hurts you, resist the urge to act out in anger and revenge. You have a *choice* in how you respond to them. Hinduism and Buddhism teach that what you send out returns to you. This is *karma*. Try to send out tolerance, even love. The Golden Rule works.

❖ When upset, choose your words carefully; you cannot take them back. Remember:

The spoken word is your master; the unspoken word, your slave.

❖ Extreme *jerks* require extreme measures:

    Step 1: Retool with humor.

    Step 2: Forgive.

    Step 3: "Kill 'em with Kindness."

    Step 4: If all else fails, lose this relationship!

❖ Pay attention to your *dreams*, even if you do not understand them. As Freud wrote, they are the *royal road to the unconscious* — a gateway to our deepest emotions, giving insight into our lives, values, and our feelings toward others.

❖ Give thanks for the miracle of *healing*. When we are injured physically, our bodies can heal. When we are injured emotionally, we can heal from that too, but it will take time. Use your *Tools* to help it along.

❖ Help yourself by *helping others*. You will reap the rewards.

❖ Be *gracious in defeat*.

❖ Tips for growing a good brain: Use time wisely, be with people, and do constructive things in a quality way. Like Aristotle said, "We are what we repeatedly do. Excellence, then, is not an act, but a habit."

❖ If you feel like *Sisyphus* pushing the rock up the hill, only to have it roll back down again, stop! Learn the First Law of Holes: if you're in one, stop digging! Step out of this frustrating cycle and reflect on what is going on. If you are in a situation that you cannot change for now, try to change yourself with an attitude adjustment.

❖ If your goal is worthy, but the *timing* is off, learn to wait. But when the time is right, you should act. As in the oceans, there is an ebb and flow to life. Hold fast to Shakespeare's wisdom:

> There is a tide in the affairs of men,
> Which, taken at the flood, leads on to fortune;
> Omitted, all the voyage of their life
> Is bound in the shallows and in miseries...
> And we must take the current when it serves,
> Or lose our ventures.

❖ Be open to *Synchronicity*. If you have an inkling that you have met someone special or found yourself in a uniquely fortuitous circumstance, make a note of it in your journal. When we are in the midst of a miracle, we cannot always see its full extent, but later we do, and it is important to remember its beginnings.

❖ This is a time of *flux*. People will enter and leave your life. Your perspectives on issues and people will evolve. Priorities will shift. With so much change, where can you find *constancy*?

- ❖ Find it by building a foundation of *truths* that you decide are important to you. Start with *Plato's Four Virtues:*

  Wisdom, Justice, Moderation, and Courage.

- ❖ Maintain a *spiritual* center where reside: *responsibility, integrity, loyalty, diligence, gratitude, altruism, tolerance, and compassion.*

- ❖ Establish *values* that transcend externals, such as beauty, intelligence, money, and social position.

- ❖ Build an *ethical code* that you can use all your life.

- ❖ Seek *eternal truths* that have stood the test of time, as they will give you a solid foundation for a good life.

- ❖ *Tell the truth with love.*

- ❖ Make *peace* with the past and *remember* those who have helped you.

- ❖ You will make *mistakes*; everyone does. Learn from them, integrate the lessons, and move on.

- ❖ Thomas Jefferson advised, "*Take things always by the smooth handle*"—i.e. in stride. Don't *worry* about the future; you can't control it. Most of the things we worry about never happen anyway. Focus on the promise of *today*, watch life unfold, and take in the miracle of it all.

- ❖ See yourself as a member of the *world*, respectful of her resources and protective of all living things. Make time to enjoy Nature, for If we lose our connection to her, we lose our humanity.

- ❖ Be a good *steward* of your country and leave it a better place than it was when you were born.

- ❖ Be *patriotic* and guard your *liberties*. President Reagan said,

"Freedom is never more than one generation from extinction."

Will you let it go down on your watch?

❖ *See Duty as a work out for your soul* — not always pleasant and often inconvenient, but doing it builds endurance, makes us strong, and helps us sleep.

❖ The ancient Greeks said that the *unexamined life is not worth living*. As you walk down the road of life, examine yours as much as you can. Keep your *Tools* in your back pocket as you seek your own individual pathway and enjoy others who are on the same road. Grab onto these years with gusto, hold fast to your ideals, and savor all the good things life will bring you! Stay on the high road and *Keep your eye on the prize!*

- Appendix -

LIST OF RESOURCES

1. National Suicide Prevention Lifeline:
   1-800-273-TALK (1-800-273-8255);
   TTY: 1-800-799-4TTY (4889).

2. Mayo Clinic's website, "What to do when someone is suicidal":
   http://www.mayoclinic.com/health/suicide/MH00058

3. General Emotional help support group: Emotions Anonymous— 12 Step Program patterned after Alcoholics Anonymous They have weekly meetings designed to help each other with emotional difficulties:
   www.emotionsanonymous.org

4. Website offering help for anxiety and depression:
   http://ecouch.anu.edu.au/welcome

5. Generalized Anxiety Disorder checklist used by clinicians to assess anxiety symptoms in patients:
   http://www.phqscreeners.com/pdfs/03_GAD-7/English.pdf

6. Depression resources:

    A. The National Institute of Mental Health's website has a wealth of information on depression, including a more expanded list of symptoms and resources for help:
http://www.nimh.nih.gov/health/publications/ depression/complete-index.shtml#pub3

    B. Depression checklist used by clinicians to assess depressive symptoms in patients:
http://depression.about.com/cs/diagnosis/l/bldep-screenquiz.htm

7. Two classic self-help books by Dr. Claire Weekes designed for people with anxiety problems:
    Hope and Help for Your Nerves and
    Peace from Nervous Suffering

8. Brief self-esteem assessment tool:
http://www.performancesolutions.nc.gov/developmentInitiatives/ CareerDevelopment/Assessments/self-esteemassesment.aspx

9. Website to help teens in abusive relationships:
    www.loveisrespect.org

10. National Teen Dating Abuse Helpline **866-331-9474:**
    TTY: 866-331-8453

11. Support and resources for GLBQ youth, including suicide prevention line:

www.thetrevorproject.org
Trevor Project Suicide Help Line at 866-488-7386

12. General resources for LGBTQ youth:
www.psych.org (American Psychiatric Association)
www.apa.org (American Psychological Association)
www.ourgap.org (Group For the Advancement of Psychiatry – click on the LGBT Committee link **www.aglp.org/gap**)

13. Student support education network of gay, lesbian, and straight youth: **www.glsen.org**

14. Groups for Alcohol and Drug Problems based on Alcoholics Anonymous model:
A. **Alcoholics Anonymous**–for adults and teens with alcohol problems. **http://www.aa.org**

B. **Teen Anon**— for teens with a drinking or drug problem **http://www.teen-anon.com/home.htm**

C. **Narcotics Anonymous**— focuses on addiction **http://www.na.org**

D. **Cocaine Anonymous: http://www.ca.org**

15. The National Institute on Drug Abuse (NIDA) and the National Institute on Alcohol Abuse and Alcoholism (NIAAA) are components of the National Institute of Health. They have pamphlets full of information on alcohol and drug abuse and links for teens, college students, and adults.

    http://www.drugabuse.gov/nidahome.html

    http://www.thecoolspot.gov

16. Help with eating disorders:
    http://www.nationaleatingdisorders.org/

17. Program for those struggling with weight:
    Take Off Pounds Sensibly (www.tops.org)

18. Career guidance:
    http://www.career-test-info-guide.com/index.html

19. PBS Frontline Program, "Inside the Teenage Brain":
    http://www.pbs.org/wgbh/pages/frontline/shows/ teenbrain/view/#rest

20. "Warning Signs of Tech Overload":
    http://topics.nytimes.com/top/features/timestopics/series/ your_brain_on_computers/index.html?scp=3&sq =Tara%20Parker%20Pope&st=cse

Keep Your Eye
on the Prize!

Whether....

Today   *or* Tomorrow!

www.keepyoureyeontheprize.org
© 2011 Barbara Long, M.D.
For additional copies, email Dr. Long at:
barbaralongmdphd@gmail.com
www.barbaralongmdphd.com
Look for Keep Your Eye On The Prize on Facebook
www.facebook.com/pages/Keep-Your-Eye-on-the-Prize/139708889411594?ref=ts

NOTES

_____

_____

_____

_____

_____

_____

_____

_____

_____

_____

_____

_____

_____

_____

_____

_____

NOTES

NOTES

NOTES

NOTES

Book Order Form

Barbara Long, M.D., Ph.D.

www.keepyoureyeontheprize.org
barbaralongmdphd@gmail.com
www.barbaralongmdphd.com

Please send me _____ copies of *Keep Your Eye on the Prize!*, at the rate of $20.00 each, plus shipping charges noted below.

Note: Please email for special rates on 25 or more books.

Name _____

Address _____

City _____ State _____ Zip_____

Shipping Charges

Quantity of Books	Shipping Charge
1	$7.00
2-3	$8.00
4-6	$9.00
7-9	$10.00
10 +	email zip code for rate